BORDER COUNTRY
CYCLE ROUTES

ABOUT THE AUTHOR

John Brewer has lived and worked in the Scottish Borders for
over 20 years. He has a passion for mountains and remote
places, and has walked and climbed in many of the major
European ranges and also in North Africa and the Canadian
Rockies and Pacific Northwest of the USA.

Seeing the potential of modern mountain bikes to access
more remote places and efficiently cover long distances, John
created the **www.bikeroutes.org.uk website**, in which he sets
out to describe and map cycle routes in southeast Scotland
and northeast England. The routes range from the more
leisurely to the more demanding, and, in fact, this guide grew
out of his search for more offbeat trails in the area…

BORDER COUNTRY
CYCLE ROUTES

by

John Brewer

CICERONE PRESS
2 POLICE SQUARE, MILNTHORPE, CUMBRIA, UK LA7 7PY
www.cicerone.co.uk

© John Brewer 2002
Reprinted 2009 (with updates)
ISBN-10: 1 85284 333 0
ISBN-13: 978 1 85284 333 5

A catalogue record for this book is available from the British Library.
Printed by KHL Printing, Singapore

Acknowledgements

Much of the inspiration for this guide came from time spent developing the website at **www.bikeroutes.org.uk** and I'm grateful to those who've contributed to the site and offered advice and feedback. I'm also grateful to Graham and Keith who have both enjoyed many memorable days out and also endured the ones that didn't go so well. Special thanks go to Joan who has accompanied me on many of the trips and been a source of encouragement throughout.

Front cover: Old rail track near Kielder, Bloody Bush Road

CONTENTS

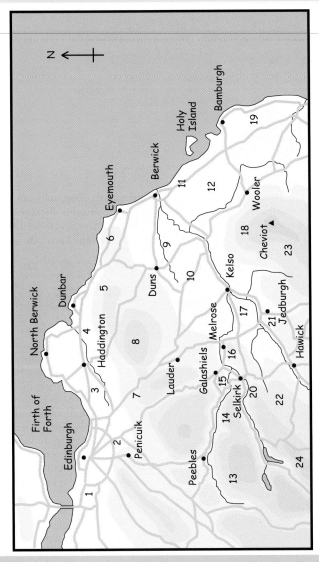

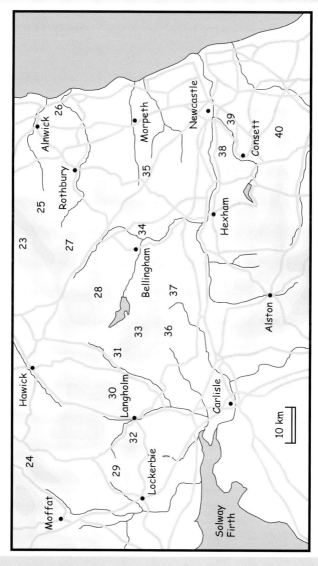

Kelso Abbey (Route 17)

Introduction

The Scottish Borders and Northumberland rank among the finest and most scenic parts of the country and this guide brings you descriptions and sketch maps of 40 original cycle routes in the area, presented in roughly north-to-south order. Most, but not all of them, have off-road sections but there is a wide variety, and if you enjoy cycling then you should be able to find something here to suit your tastes. Some of the routes are content to wander along leafy lanes and through quiet villages, while others are more demanding and will take you to wild and remote hills and mountains.

This part of the country is often overlooked by tourists and yet its secrets are there to be discovered by those who take time to seek them out. The coastline varies from craggy cliffs, like those found at St Abbs Head, to the miles of golden sand that is Druridge Bay. Inland, the coastal plains give way to upland areas such as the Lammermuirs, the Southern Uplands, the Cheviots and the Pennines, all of which have their own characteristics and all of which offer their own challenges.

The Northumberland National Park, in particular, is in stark contrast to its neighbour on the other side of the country, the Lake District National Park. The scenery in both is quite stunning, but whereas in the Lake District it's often difficult to get away from crowds, in the Northumberland Park you can often cycle all day and seldom see a soul. The same can be said of parts of the Southern Uplands, and this area has its own unique blend of both isolation and charm in equal measure.

Of course, many prefer more leisurely trails and enjoy exploring the rich history of the towns and villages. The Border country has a bloody and violent past, and this is clearly reflected in the variety of architecture to be found here – abbeys and churches for the pious and the poor; castles and keeps for the reivers and the rich.

Cycling is one of the best and most efficient ways to get around the countryside, and a bike will get you to places that you may not otherwise be able to get to easily. In a similar vein, walking along forest tracks wouldn't be my favourite pastime, but using them to reach fairly inaccessible places by bike is an altogether different matter.

Modern bikes have come a long way in terms of design and materials in recent years and are quite different machines to those that many of us remember from our childhood years. Innovation doesn't, of itself, guarantee improvement, but today's bikes are a good deal lighter and much easier to ride than many of the old steel beasts that I remember.

All the routes are circular and have a suggested starting point, but obviously it may suit some people to start from a different location, depending on where they access it from. A summary description indicates the length and difficulty of the route, and this should help you to decide whether it is suitable for your ability and your bike. Outdoor skills are needed for some of the more challenging excursions, and you may need to exercise some caution when choosing these. Occasionally you may have to get off and push for, hopefully, a short distance but none of the routes sets out to be a test of endurance. Sometimes there is an alternative way of cycling a particular part of the route, and these are shown in italic type. Places shown on the sketch maps are highlighted in bold type in the text to aid orientation.

A small number of the trips involve cycling on beaches and, although this can be tremendous fun, there are obvious problems here – salt water and sand are not bike-friendly. However, alternatives are suggested if you don't want to use the beach and, in any event, it may be best to leave these sections for the end of the day so that any sand can be washed off before it does damage.

The time spent on main roads has been minimised as far as possible, though sometimes it simply isn't possible to avoid them altogether. No attempt has been made to put a time on the routes as there are just too many variables. In any case, these are meant to be leisurely trips, so take your time, stop and look at whatever takes your fancy and, most of all, enjoy!

Route Grading and Distances

Routes in the guide are graded on a scale of 1 to 5 in increasing order of difficulty. The grade is purely subjective but tries to take into account the length of the route, the terrain, whether there are any strenuous sections – for example, if you need to push for a while – and whether it involves steep climbs.

Grade 1 routes should be reasonably short, fairly leisurely and present no real difficulties. At the other end of the scale, grade 5 routes might be quite long, involve steep climbs, travel through more challenging or isolated areas, or require some walking with your bike – likely as not, there will be a combination of these features.

Distances are approximate. Generally speaking, I've used 'track' to mean anything not on a public road, but where a 'track' becomes a 'path' is a little more difficult to define. Sometimes it's the nature of the surface – a path may be a little rougher than a track – but mostly it's because a path will be narrower and you'll probably need to cycle single file.

Getting Around

Despite the proximity of major towns and cities like Edinburgh, Carlisle and Newcastle, public transport in the area is particularly poor. Although the main east coast rail line passes through Scottish Borders, there isn't a single rail station in the entire region. Access by train to the Borders is therefore limited to Edinburgh and other towns such as Lockerbie in the west, Berwick in the east and Dunbar in East Lothian.

South of the border, the east coast rail line has a number of stations, as does the Newcastle to Carlisle line. Some bus operators may carry bikes, but whether you're travelling by train or bus, you would really need to check in advance to see whether this is feasible or not.

The nearest airports are at Edinburgh and Newcastle and in both cases they are quite a way out from the city centre, though Newcastle airport does at least have a rail link.

Accommodation

All the main towns have hotels, and indeed tourism is seen as an increasingly important element of the region's economy. Similarly, bed and breakfast accommodation is widely available, though you may wish to book ahead for the more popular places and those near to the long-distance routes – mentioned later – which pass through the area.

Youth Hostels operated by the YHA and the Scottish YHA are another option, and can vary from the simple- and basic-category hostels to the more luxurious Grade 1 variety as found in, for example, Edinburgh. The price, of course, reflects the accommodation provided.

Campsites, too, vary from the cheap and cheerful to the more expensive. Nowadays I'm more inclined to pay a little more for a decent site with reasonable facilities and, more importantly, some expectation of a peaceful night ahead. A sign of the times, I suppose, but it's all a matter of taste.

I mention bothies with some reluctance. If you follow the routes in

Scott's View, the River Tweed and the Eildon Hills (Route 16)

this guide you'll come across four. Two of them – Yearning Saddles and Auchope Rigg – are little more than shelters and, being on the Pennine Way, are quite well known. The other two are not so well known, but quite delightful in their own way. I've used bothies in the Highlands and have always appreciated that there's a code of ethics involved in doing so. Of course, they are there for people to use but my only concern is that those who do so recognise that these are special places and should be treated as such. Leave them in as good a condition as you find them – indeed, you should try and leave them in a better condition than you find them.

WHEN TO GO

Prevailing weather systems come from the west and, generally speaking, the eastern side of the country gets less rainfall then the west. Of course, the weather can be fickle at any time of year and there are never any guarantees.

Cycling is really a year-round activity and, for the visitor, it's well worth considering going out of season. A good spell in October will reveal rich autumn colours, while spring brings out the early flowers. Winter days are short, but clear air and snow on the tops can make for some breathtaking views.

At any time of the year good weather is a bonus, but sometimes it's refreshing to just go riding in the rain, come what may. Take the opportunity to unwind and let the stresses of modern living simply melt away.

Equipment

Most of the routes in this guide are on, or near, roads where help is to hand in case of emergency. Some of them, however, take you through fairly remote areas where mechanical problems could cause real difficulty. Nor can mobile phone users be sure that they will be able to use them in an emergency, though coverage is improving. In other words, it's best to plan to be as self-sufficient as possible.

Equally, some routes need mountain (and sometimes winter) gear and it's all too easy to get caught out. Normal cycle clothing is quite unsuitable for these conditions and more specialised outdoor clothing would be a better choice. Other typical equipment for mountainous areas might include a compass, headtorch, whistle, first-aid kit and so on.

I've always felt that there's really no option but to buy good quality tools, even if it costs a little more. The last thing you want in difficult circumstances is spanners that bend or break, or soft-headed screwdrivers that simply don't do the job. Some of the multi-tool kits are excellent but, generally speaking, you get what you pay for. A good chain splitter is, I reckon, essential.

Whether to use a bum bag, rucksack or rack-mounted bag is really a matter of personal preference and may also depend on how much you're carrying. I find it more comfortable to avoid wearing a rucksack when cycling if at all possible, and usually use a rack-mounted bag which can convert into a small rucksack if necessary.

Despite what some say about letting air out of your tyres on soft ground for extra grip, I'm not actually convinced that it's the best thing to do. One reason for this is the fact that soft tyres are more susceptible to 'pinch' punctures. If you do have a puncture, of course, then you really don't want to have to fix it – at least, not there and then – so a spare tube is essential kit. My experience is that 'glueless' patches do work, but on the other hand, I've also used 'ordinary' glue and patches to do a running repair on a tyre wall that burst; at least one that was good enough to get the victim home.

Lastly, a couple of other items have found their way onto my 'essentials' checklist. One is a midge hood, and if you've ever tried to carry out fiddly repairs in a dank and windless wood where the local midge and fly population think that Christmas has arrived early…well, you'll probably know what I mean. The hoods weigh next to nothing, squash into the teeniest of corners and can save a whole lot of misery – vanity is decidedly not an issue in situations like this! And having done those repairs and ended up with greasy, oily hands? Well I always take a tiny plastic container of washing-up liquid, and if that sounds vain I can only say that such a simple solution really can make a difference when these things happen, as they inevitably will.

ENVIRONMENTAL ISSUES

Off-road routes raise important issues of their own. Many of them see very little usage, but others can be busier. Some pass through fragile environments, albeit on marked tracks, but in general terms it seems clear that we should all do what we can to minimise the potential for damage – it really isn't a smart move to leave evidence of your passing in the form of skid damage and chewed-up sections of track.

While some of the larger estates are happy to let cyclists and walkers have access to their land, others are less so, and it's worth considering how to avoid problems and confrontation which might ultimately lead to access restrictions. Hill farmers, for example, are particularly sensitive during the lambing season, so care should be taken to stay on marked trails at that time. By the same token, cyclists should be sensitive to other country users and also landowners whose interests might include hunting and shooting, whatever your own opinions on the issue.

HISTORICAL NOTE

I don't claim to have any specialist historical knowledge, but I have learned a lot while researching this book and I'll confess to it having kindled more than just a passing interest. Cycling through some of this largely unspoilt countryside, I was struck by just how little I knew about it, and about the people who made it what it is. I've still barely scratched the surface, but for me, it helps to paint a broader canvas when you can relate what you find in dusty tomes to the evidence that you can see around you.

An example: when I first passed through Bewcastle, some years ago, I'd never even heard of the Bewcastle Cross. Beautiful landscape, but I'd cycled right past the small churchyard where the cross had stood for hundreds of years, going right back to the so-called Dark Ages. It happens that this is also the site of a Roman fort which existed even hundreds of years before that, and you can't help but wonder how such an isolated place was the focus of so much activity.

So, no history lessons from me, but just a few pointers to features and places of interest that some of these routes will take you to. They won't be to everyone's taste, of course, but the option is there and it's for you to decide.

Hadrian's Wall stretches from the Solway Firth to the Tyne estuary and must be seen as a tremendous feat of Roman engineering. The Roman influence, of course, is evident north of the border too. Dere Street, for example, forced a route from York to Edinburgh and supplied forts like Trimontium, near Melrose, on the way. New remains and artefacts continue to be discovered, and several routes in the guide pass by major sites of interest including Vindolanda, Trimontium, Ebchester, Lanchester and Hadrian's Wall itself.

Evidence of the more substantial stone structures of the early and late Middle Ages is much more prevalent. Ancient abbeys and churches can still be seen, as can the more humble fortified towers and castles that were built to protect people in those bloody and violent times. Preston Tower, on the Beadnell route, is one of my favourites – it's not right in the heart of reivers' country, but it has a lot of tales to tell and is well worth a visit.

More recent history has left its mark in a number of ways throughout the region. Scars from the industrial past are everywhere to be seen in this corner of northeast England, including old mine workings, collieries, steel mills and the railways that used to support them. The Tyne Valley, Beamish and Deerness Valley routes all demonstrate this and more.

In the Lothians, too, mining played a large part in the economy, particularly around Tranent, while the Borders had its very own thriving textile industry. Nowadays just a few mills are still in production, some stand as empty shells and others have gone for ever. Galashiels, Selkirk and Hawick are the centres for what remains of the industry.

Old rail route near Rowlands Gill, Derwent Valley (Route 39)

Along the coast, too, from the Forth to the Tyne, the traditional fishing industry has declined to an extent and some smaller ports are all but empty. Eyemouth, on the other hand, has recently had major improvements carried out to its harbour. The Coldingham route allows the contrast to be drawn between the 'old' port of St Abbs and the 'new' port at Eyemouth. It also takes you through the timeless tourist resort of Coldingham, complete with its painted huts on the beach.

LEGAL ISSUES

The law relating to access for off-road cyclists is quite different in England and Scotland. In England, cyclists are allowed to used bridle-ways, by-ways and roads used as a public path (RUPPs), but in each case they must always give way to horse riders and pedestrians. There is no right of access to cyclists on footpaths in England.

By way of contrast, Scotland introduced an Outdoor Access Code in 2005 giving cyclists, walkers and other outdoor users the right of access to most areas of the country. Those rights are accompanied by a responsibility to use the countryside in a sensible way. Indeed, the word 'responsible' occurs frequently in the legislation and is, of course, open to wide interpretation.

Landowners, too, have a responsibility not just to allow access, but also to facilitate it. You may still come across padlocked gates from time to time and it's fair to say that not everyone has welcomed the changes. But changes there have been, and it's difficult to see how they could be reversed now.

In short, it seems like the best advice is to try and avoid confrontation with landowners – long-term damage to relations is in no one's interest.

All the routes in this guide have been checked for legality as far as is possible, but we have to note that things do change and any feedback regarding potential access difficulties would be appreciated. Useful information will be posted on the updates area for this guidebook on the Cicerone website and also kept on file for future reprints.

Maps

For all but the easiest routes, you should really take a decent map with you. It has already been mentioned that some of these routes pass through remote areas where mapreading skills are essential, and I can recall occasions when the cloud has come down and there's been no choice but to get the compass out and use it to navigate. The rounded and featureless terrain found in many areas hereabouts can be particularly confusing and simply serves to emphasise the point.

The best general purpose maps, in my view, are the Ordnance Survey 1:50000 'Landranger' series and these will be sufficient for most purposes. The OS also produce an excellent 1:25000 'Outdoor Leisure' series covering areas such as Hadrian's Wall, Kielder, the Cheviots and the Tweed Valley. They're double-sided and contain a lot of useful detail. The information at the start of each route gives the relevant OS map number for the ride.

For areas that I use regularly, I'll sometimes cut up a map into smaller, more manageable, sections that will fit into a shirt pocket and either laminate them or cover them in transparent sticky plastic.

LONG-DISTANCE ROUTES

Several long-distance cycle routes cross the region, among them the Tweed Cycleway, the Four Abbeys Route, two Sustrans coast to coast routes – the C2C and the Reivers Cycle Route – and part of the east coast National Cycle Network that passes through Northumberland and the south of Scotland to Edinburgh.

There's also a number of walking and horse riding routes, some sections of which may be used by cyclists – the Pennine Way, St Cuthbert's Way, the Southern Upland Way and the Border County Ride.

CYCLE HIRE AND SPARES

Cycling is increasing in popularity and more facilities are being developed to cater for the demand. Many towns will have cycle dealers able to supply spares, and specialist companies offering cycling-related holidays are also making an appearance.

Visitor Information Offices are probably the best source for local details. Many of them will also be able to offer information about cycling facilities in the area and possibly provide leaflets indicating marked routes.

CONTACT INFORMATION

Visitor Information Offices can often offer useful local advice and some have route guides and/or leaflets. Phone numbers and websites, where they exist, are listed here.

Northumbria Tourism
www.visitnorthumberland.com

Scottish Borders Tourism
www.scot-borders.co.uk

Visitor Information Offices open all year

Alnwick	01665 511333
Bellingham	01434 220616
Berwick	01289 330733
Corbridge	01434 632815
Craster	01665 576007

The Bewcastle Cross (Route 33)

Hawick	01835 863170
Hexham	01434 652220
Jedburgh	01835 863170
Kelso	01835 863170
Melrose	01835 863170
Morpeth	01670 500700
Otterburn	01830 520093
Peebles	01835 863170
Rothbury	01669 620887
Wooler	01668 282123

Otterburn Range Control
(to check access to the MOD range)
01830 520569
www.otterburnranges.co.uk

WEBSITES:
Some websites are listed here, but with the usual disclaimer that the nature of the internet is such that websites come and go, so the existence of the links can't be guaranteed. On the other hand, information on the sites may be more up to date than printed material...

www.sustrans.org.uk Sustrans: the National Cycling Network
www.ctc.org.uk Cyclists' Touring Club
www.visitkielder.com Kielder Water and Forest Park
www.7stanes.gov.uk the 7stanes mountain bike trails
www.northumberland.gov.uk search for "Holy Island" to check the tides
www.jmt.org The John Muir Trust
www.mountainbothies.org.uk Mountain Bothies Association
www.bikeroutes.org.uk ...which gave rise to this guide...

1. Ratho

Distance:	**19 miles**
OS Maps:	**Landranger 65**
Start:	**Cramond**
Grade:	**1**
Surface:	**road** **6 miles**
	track **13 miles**

The River Almond rises in the hills between Edinburgh and Glasgow. It crosses an industrial landscape, and then cuts a more leisurely line right through the middle of the flat expanse that is Edinburgh Airport before heading down to join the Forth at Cramond. This route starts by following the Almond upstream from Cramond and uses cycle tracks, minor roads and the towpath on the Union Canal to make a trip which contains much beauty and tranquillity and yet is only a few miles from Edinburgh city centre.

Cramond village is a picturesque spot. There's a pub, a waterside cafe by the harbour, a beach and, of course, Cramond Island is just offshore. When the tide is out you can stroll across to it. Beyond the island you can see Inchcolm Island and the Fife coast. On the other side of the River Almond is the Dalmeny Estate and, while the estate isn't accessible from Cramond itself, the Round the Forth Cycling Route (NCR76) does pass through it.

Cramond is easily accessible along the coast from Granton to the east. There's also a well-signed parking area.

A walking/cycling route leads up the glen to Cramond Brig. It's a popular stroll so be aware that pedestrians have right of way. There are a few steps by a weir and the remains of an old mill, but this is just a taste of what's to come because soon you'll need to carry your bike up a steep flight of seventy-odd wooden steps, go along a little, and carry it down a similar number on the other side. It would be a shame to miss out on the ride up this glen simply because of the steps. How you might avoid them on the return leg is explained but, of course, you might simply want to start the route at Cramond Brig instead.

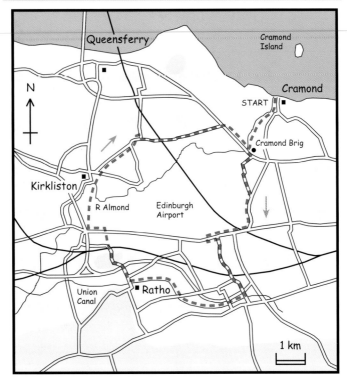

Eventually you'll find yourself on Dowies Mill Lane, and turning right at the end of it will take you over **Cramond Brig**. The bridge has inscriptions indicating that repairs were carried out on a number of occasions, the oldest being in 1687. They've lasted well though, so cross the bridge and take the road behind the Cramond Brig Hotel to join the main Queensferry Road. Turn left to head towards the city and cross the 'new' bridge. You only stay with the main road for two or three hundred yards and there is a wide pavement if you prefer. Take the first turning on the right into Cammo Road.

Purists might wonder if it's possible to avoid the main road alto-gether…well it is, but it's a bit awkward. Don't cross Cramond Brig but look instead for a path to the left of a cottage which leads towards a play area. Bear right and try to stay near the riverbank as it passes under the 'new' road bridge and then force a route upwards to emerge in a housing scheme. It can be done, but I only mention it for the adventurous…

At the bottom of Cammo Road there is an imposing gateway to the Cammo Estate. A small visitor centre is housed in the lodge and has information about the estate. Turn left to follow a lane heading south. As it passes a small car park, the obvious Cammo Tower is over to your right and now sits there as an empty shell. The lane leads up to the main road where a cycle track heads along to the Maybury roundabout.

The cycle track continues alongside the A8 Glasgow road and you need to follow it as far as the RBS Bridge over the main road. Cross the bridge and pass by the RBS Headquarters to pick up Gogar Station Road to the left. Away from the traffic now, this leafy lane is less frantic and offers a welcome relief. Further on, cross a railway then bear left to go over a motorway and reach an access path down to the **Union Canal**.

A lot a work and funding has gone into making improvements to the towpath, and it's really made a difference to the often muddy track that I used to know and love. There's a good surface now, and you can enjoy the varied wildlife and open scenery as you cruise easily along to **Ratho**. The Bridge Inn is a popular haunt and is also the departure point for leisure cruises by barge along the canal.

Take the road heading north to cross the motorway and climb uphill for a way. You'll be rewarded with fine views across to Fife from the top. Drop downhill but look for a cycle track on the right just before the railway. This is the 'old' road and it meets the A8 just by another footbridge. Cross the bridge and you're heading for the Newbridge roundabout on the cycle track.

To escape the chaos and noise, look for where a track veers off to the right just by a footbridge over the M9 to follow the course of an old railway to Kirkliston and Dalmeny. Within minutes you've left motorways behind and you're in open country. In a couple of miles or so you cross over two roads. Just over the second bridge you should leave the cycle route and cut down to the road just west of Carlowrie Farm. Two miles brings you to Queensferry Road again and the bridge takes you over it and onto the 'old' road down to Cramond Brig.

Cammo Tower, Edinburgh

You can follow the outward route down the glen and back to Cramond. If you'd prefer to avoid the carry up and down steps then you should look for a narrow track off to the right a couple of hundred yards before you get to the foot of the steps. It runs alongside a garden and then joins Peggy's Mill Road which leads easily to the main Whitehouse Road. Turn left and the route back to **Cramond** village is obvious enough from here.

2. Roslin

Distance:	**13 miles**
OS Map:	**Landranger 66**
Start:	**Eskbank**
Grade:	**3**
Surface:	**road 4 miles**
	track 7 miles
	path 2 miles

A shortish route, but quite demanding in places as it weaves a delightfully improbable line through some of the lesser-known parts of Midlothian. The 1:50000 map isn't really up to the job, so actually following the route could be quite challenging at times.

Start at the former **Eskbank** Station. To find it, go to the Eskbank roundabout at (325 667) and take the A768 signed for Loanhead. The old station building is just a few yards from the roundabout on your left.

A surfaced cycle route heads south from the station along the old rail track. Jewel and Esk College is over to your left. After half a mile or so, look for the right turn that takes you to a footbridge over the A7. Cycle over the bridge and you need to find a grassy route leaving the cycle track after a couple of hundred yards. It runs behind some houses to meet the A6094 road to Howgate. Go straight across into a cul-de-sac.

The road changes to a track and there's a golf course on the right. Follow the track as it crosses part of the golf course to come out onto what is actually the A768 Loanhead road again. Turn left and head down the hill for Lasswade, cross the North Esk and turn immediately left over the bridge. The next part of the route is a little trickier.

As the road swings to the right and starts to go steeply uphill, look for a footpath on the left which also heads uphill following alongside a stone wall. Emerge into a clearing with good views of the viaduct below. Continue along the narrow lane to meet a minor road just at a bend. The route continues to the left, through trees and sometimes between high stone walls, to meet another road.

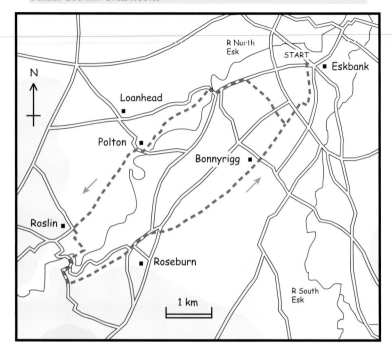

Go straight across to drop steeply downhill beside a wall. There are some steps at the bottom. The path opens out now and there are fields to the left and right and a round tower some way up the hill. The singletrack passes a large sandstone building and follows the north bank of the river to eventually reach a bridge and weir. This is the **Polton** war memorial.

Some thirty yards to your right, at the end of a low wall, is the start of a path that leads steeply and uncomfortably upwards. There are steps but this is hard work and you'll need a sense of humour as you haul yourself up them.

The trail emerges into more open woodland to pass along a narrow ridge which has steep drops on both sides. There are good views down into the glen and you need to negotiate some steps in places. The route heads down a little now, then up again to join a wider track, climbing further through the woodland. Bilston Glen is to your right.

The track improves, there are trees to the right and open views to the left as you're fairly high above the north bank of the river. A monument commemorates the battle of Roslin, fought in 1303, and a noticeboard gives further details of those events. On that occasion, and despite being outnumbered, the Scots under Comyn defeated the invading English army led by Sir John Segrave in what was by all accounts a violent and bloody encounter.

Behind the noticeboard, a path leads down to where the battle is supposed to have taken place – it isn't too clear to me just exactly where that is, but there's certainly some scope for exploration if you have time. Your route goes straight on. It's a surfaced road now and you'll pass the Roslin Institute – birthplace of Dolly the sheep – over to the right, on the way to **Roslin** village. The village, along with the trail that you've just followed, has a rural charm that belies its location right in the heart of Midlothian.

The road on the left is signed for Rosslyn Chapel, an impressive structure built in 1446 by William St Clair, the third and last Prince of Orkney. It is famed for its richly ornate carved pillars, among other things, and is rightly popular with visitors to the area. Just before the chapel, turn right down a path and head for the castle. There's a graveyard on the left – turn left following a sign for Polton. Look for steps down to the right just as you reach a stone archway at the castle. Keep the castle above and to your left as you head down through the trees to a small bridge over the river.

Cross the bridge and bear right to go through a car park and turn left onto the road. The castle comes more into view in the trees over to the left after a couple of hundred yards or so. Look for a turning on the right signed for 'Rosslea'. Follow this road up and left to pass a white cottage. Access to the cycle route – the old Penicuik to Bonnyrigg rail line – is by a small gate on the left as you reach the bridge.

The line rises gently as it pulls out of the wooded glen and into open country. Reaching a main road, cross it to find the cycle route continuing on that side of the road for a while before veering off to the right. When you arrive at the former **Bonnyrigg** Station, the continuation of the cycle route isn't obvious. Go to the end of the 'platform' then straight across the road into a newish housing scheme. You'll pick up the route again after a few yards and it's a breeze now to join the outward route from **Eskbank**.

3. Pencaitland

Distance:	**30 miles**
OS Map:	**Landranger 66**
Start:	**Musselburgh**
Grade:	**2**
Surface:	**road 18 miles**
	track 12 miles

An old coach road, a couple of disused rail lines, classic views over the Forth and parts of the East Lothian Coastal Route are all features of this trip. It works its way inland from Musselburgh to Haddington, then uses an old rail route from there to Longniddry and follows a coastal route back to the start.

Musselburgh is where the Esk flows into the Forth and, indeed, at one time it was called Eskmouth. It's a lively and bustling town, particularly on race days. There's a car park by the river on Olive Hall Road at (342 726). It's not the only one, but it is fairly central. The town is also close to two rail stations.

From the car park go to the traffic lights and take a sharp right on the road signed for Inveresk. Follow this round and you'll be heading uphill out of town and past a school. Inveresk Gardens are on the right and, shortly after passing them, turn left onto Crookston Road.

As you leave suburbia and make friends with open fields, you can't fail to notice the hill up ahead upon which sits **Falside Castle**, extensively restored in recent times. This is an old coach route, and if it wasn't for the new section of the A1 it would take a direct line up the hill to pass just to the right of the castle. There's now a slight detour, though, and when you get to the A1 the cycle route is signed and you need to cross over the main road by a bridge.

You're looking now for the left turn that is the continuation of the route. It's a hard pull up here but the views get better as you go – towards Edinburgh and right across the Forth into Fife.

Just past the castle the road becomes a track and aims across towards North Elphinstone farm, about a mile away. At the far end of

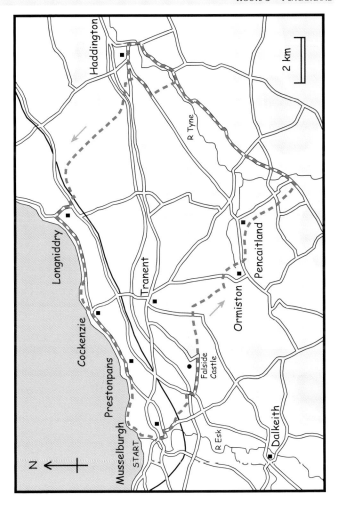

the farm buildings look for a track on the right that heads downhill. After 500m go left at a T-junction then right towards **Ormiston**. The track crosses the old Pencaitland railway, and access to what is now a

Traprain Law, East Lothian

cycle/walkway is just over the bridge and on the left. It's two miles to **Pencaitland** – make sure that you take the right fork just after passing under the B6371 – and about the same distance again to the end of the cycleway.

At West Saltoun you take to the back roads on a fairly direct course towards Haddington and passing through typical East Lothian countryside – rich farmland and cottages with distinctive red-tiled roofs. When you reach Westfield farm there's a choice, depending on whether you want to go into **Haddington** or take a shorter route avoiding the town centre.

To go through town simply follow the road round, crossing the River Tyne, and this will bring you into the main street and busy market square. There are plenty of shops, pubs and so on. Make sure that you leave the town on the B6471 and look for the sign pointing to access the cycle route at (502 738) as described below.

To avoid the town centre and cut off a mile or so from the total distance, then look for a footbridge over the Tyne just past Westfield. Cross the bridge and follow the track for a mile to the main road. Take the road towards the town centre for about a mile and then look for

Clerkington Road on the left leading into a housing scheme. When the 'main' road through the estate swings to the right, carry straight on and down a short connecting path to come out on the B6471 at (502 738) just opposite the access point for the Haddington to Longniddry cycle route, which is straight ahead and over the bridge.

The cycle route leaves the town, passes under the A1 and, climbing only gently, takes on the tranquillity of the countryside – passing sometimes through sheltered wooded cuttings and sometimes through open fields. Views open up once more to the Forth and eventually the route runs alongside the main east coast rail line as it approaches **Longniddry** Station. You don't want to carry your bike over the footbridge, so just before reaching the platform, turn left and back on yourself to take a track that goes down and under the railway to bring you out on the road. Take the main road for a short way down to the shore and turn left to run alongside Seton Sands.

In all honesty it can't be said that this stretch of coastline is stunning but it does have its odd moments. Look out for signs for the East Lothian Coastal Route. Port Seton harbour is worth a detour and there's a path along the waterfront from here to **Cockenzie** Harbour. There's no real alternative to using the road past the power station, though, and on through **Prestonpans**.

Approaching **Musselburgh**, the Coastal Route invites you to follow the sea wall which skirts round to emerge where the Esk flows into the Forth. From here, paths take you along the riverbank and back to the car park.

4. Garvald

Distance:	**37 miles**
OS Map:	**Landranger 67**
Start:	**Dunbar**
Grade:	**3**
Surface:	**road** **28.5 miles/34.5 miles**
	track **5 miles/1 mile**
	path **3.5 miles/1.5 miles**

*This is a tremendous route which is never strenuous but always
full of interest. Among other things, it passes through parts of the
John Muir Country Park and there's an optional 'spur' to go and
visit St Baldred's Cradle – if you want to avoid this then you can
reduce the overall distance by five miles. Although most of the
off-road sections can be avoided, to do so would mean missing
out on many of the best features of this trip – in any event, the
tracks and paths are generally on good surfaces throughout.*

Dunbar is a busy town and worth taking some time to explore. There
are the ruins of Dunbar Castle, originally built on a site by the harbour
in the 13th century, although most of what you now see is probably
16th century. The harbour itself is always colourful and in the High
Street you'll find the John Muir House, birthplace of the Scottish con-
servationist and now a museum.

At the west end of the town is a car park on Shore Road (662 787)
and the route is described from there.

Turn right out of the car park and cross the main road to go past a
hospital and under the railway. When you reach the main A1 go straight
across and take a right fork for Pitcox. A little further on is **Stenton**, quite
a picturesque village with its church and what was the tron, or market-
place weighing machine.

As you leave the village, fork left past the primary school and climb
gently towards Ruchlaw Mains. Pressmennan Wood on your left has a
forest trail and picnic area. About half a mile past Newmains there's a
track on the left for **Stoneypath Tower**. The tower was probably built
in the 1490s and is in a commanding position overlooking the glen
through which flows Whittingehame Water. Take the path on the left
leading down to the stream and follow it through woodland, crossing
three small bridges, before it brings you into Garvald village.

*This off-road section can be avoided but it does involve a detour
and may be more effort than it's worth. The distance figures that are
quoted for the alternative route assume that you do follow this route but
perhaps walk the section through the woods.*

Garvald is a pleasant village with a pub. There's a fairly steep, but
short, haul as you leave. Turn right at the main road, heading back
towards Dunbar, but only for a mile or so before turning left for Papple.
As you crest the ridge views open up towards the Bass Rock, Arthur's

Cramond harbour and Cobble Cottage (Route 1)

John Muir Country Park at Dunbar (Route 4)

The causeway to Holy Island, Lindisfarne (Route 11)

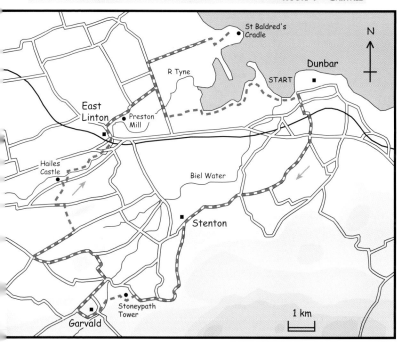

Seat and across the Forth to Fife. Traprain Law is the obvious volcanic plug just a mile to the north. Also, at what is probably the high point of this route, is a monument to a Major James Balfour. As with many structures like this, however, we're not told much about the either the person or the significance, if any, of this particular location.

Roll down to the crossroads and turn right towards Traprain. You may see some climbers on the crag; it is a deservedly popular venue, partly because of its south-facing aspect. As you draw level with the hill look for a track on the left signposted by the Scottish Rights of Way Society. It rises gently then falls to meet another road in about half a mile.

Again, avoiding this necessitates a lengthy detour and the mileage figures assume that this part of the route is followed.

Turn left and just a few yards on the right is another track sign-posted for Hailes Castle. Go through a narrow gate and follow it down to the road.

This section is easy to avoid if you go along the road for half a mile then take a right turn back towards the castle.

Built by Hugo de Gourlay in the 1290s, **Hailes Castle** is one of the oldest in Scotland. Like many others, it has a violent history and has changed ownership several times according to the whims of patronage and victory in battle. Following Mary Queen of Scots' abduction she was held here briefly before being taken to Dunbar. Looking around the tranquil scene nowadays, it's difficult to picture the horrors that went on all those years ago.

Just a hundred yards or so along the road is a track, again sign-posted by the Scottish Rights of Way Society, which crosses the river and follows its north bank on a good path to East Linton. There is a point where you'll need to carry your bike up and down some steps. The trail passes underneath the main A1 via a gallery and leads into **East Linton** village.

Avoid this section by following the road to where it meets the A1 then cross straight over it and down into the village.

There's a charm about the place and you might want to take a few minutes just to sit and watch, well, whatever passes by. When the time comes, though, leave the village and look for signs to **Preston Mill**, off to the right and less than a mile. The mill is owned by the National Trust for Scotland. The buildings date from the 1700s but there has been a mill on the site since the 16th century. If you're using the 1:50000 OS map then you'll see a picture of it on the front cover.

Take the road along to Tyninghame now; a village of curious archi-tecture and one that's unnaturally neat and tidy. Where it meets the A168 the route out to St Baldred's Cradle turns left, but only for half a mile to Limetree Walk at the end of which is a small car park. Note the impressive, but private, Tyninghame House over to the right.

This is now part of the John Muir Country Park. You could explore the area on foot but there is a track leading southeast and, after a couple of hundred yards, a branch off to the left. This is the one that takes you to **St Baldred's Cradle**, but it's also worth investigating the route that goes straight ahead – take a stroll out to the spit running southwest. The sands and saltmarsh areas around the bay are a delight for birdwatchers.

Not much seems to be known of the eponymous saint, though some say he lived the life of a hermit on Bass Rock until his death in AD 608. St Baldred's Chapel is the oldest building on the Rock. St Baldred's Cradle on the other hand is…well, you'll just have to see what you make of it. Whatever the origin of the name, it is a fine place to be and its mood changes both with the weather and the state of the tide.

Go back the way you came, heading for the A1. Shortly after crossing the Tyne look for a track on the left leading towards its outlet into the bay. This, too, is part of the Country Park and you can follow a good trail right round the bay. You pass some old concrete wartime sea defences and it's possible to take a number of trails through the woods, round to Belhaven Bay and back to the car park.

You can avoid this last section by going straight to the A1 where there is a cycleway alongside the road. This will take you along to the Dunbar turn-off from where it's a mile and a half back to the car park.

5. Olhamstocks

Distance:	32 miles
OS Map:	Landranger 67
Start:	Ellemford Bridge, near Cranshaws
Grade:	3
Surface:	road 28 miles/31 miles
	track 2.5 miles/0.5 mile
	path 1.5 miles/0.5 mile

Olhamstocks is a small village tucked in the northeastern foothills of the Lammermuirs. The route starts, however, a few miles inland, and while there are a number of possibilities it seemed that somewhere along the Cranshaws road would be a good choice. In particular, it means that the steep haul over to Abbey St Bathans comes early in the day rather than at the end of it.

Ellemford Bridge crosses **Whiteadder Water** by a phone box and the Southern Upland Way passes nearby. The road rises gently before dropping down to the **Abbey St Bathans** junction. There are only two roads into the village and this is the approach from the south. What an approach it is, though, as the road climbs steeply for half a mile before the gradient eases and you emerge into more open hillside. Pause to catch your breath and take in the views.

Of the ancient abbey of Bernadines, founded in 1170 and dedicated to St Bathan, there is no trace now. The village does, however, boast some tea rooms and a church but no shops. As you roll into it, it is possible to cut a corner by crossing the bridge by the tea rooms, but instead go a few yards further, turn right to pass the church and cross the river by a fine suspension bridge.

The Southern Upland Way also passes this way but this section crosses Whiteburn Farm and is off-limits to cyclists. Follow the bank of the river along a path passing the other bridge before starting to head uphill through trees. The path emerges into open country before going downhill to meet a rough track. The track has a fairly loose surface and trends upwards, away from the river, to meet a road after about a mile.

NB. This last section is not really suitable for road bikes but it can be avoided by taking the other road out of the village as it goes uphill to pass Whiteburn Farm.

Turning left, now, there's an undulating stretch of road for three miles or so before heading uphill to (almost) the top of Ecclaw Hill. The wide expanse of sea to the north holds your gaze.

As you gather speed downhill make sure not to miss the left turn for **Olhamstocks** by a group of cottages. There's more downhill to come, but then the road climbs up slightly to enter the village. Small well-kept cottages and gardens give a distinct appearance to the place. It has a village green but no shop and no pub.

Moving along to the church you'll find a curious tale. In the churchyard is the tiny Gravewatcher's House. The church itself is 14th century but the Gravewatcher's House was built in 1824 because Mrs Agnes Moore, the Minister's wife, 'was much alarmed by the reports of bodies being dug up to supply the Edinburgh medical students'.

The road continues up the valley but reverts to track when you pass Stottencleugh Farm. It crosses a stream bed and becomes fairly indistinct for a short way – you should aim for an obvious track which rises to pass just to the right of the cottage on the hill ahead. There follows a pleasant run down the valley now to Thurston Mains where you turn left.

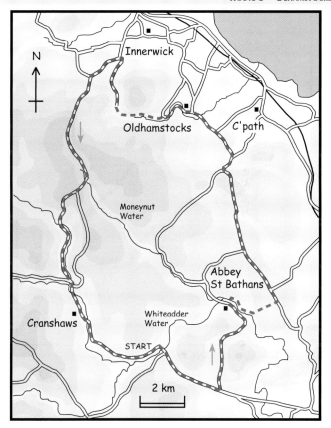

NB. It is certainly possible to avoid this short off-road section, but to do so would involve a considerable detour via Innerwick and the associated height gain/loss. For the effort involved, and given that this is reasonably flat and gentle grassy farm track/path, it might be worth considering simply pushing the bike over any problematic areas.

Don't be fooled by the gentle gradient because the serious climb is yet to come. It starts at Elmscleugh and, like it or not, you can see what

The Gravewatcher's House, Olhamstocks

needs doing as you head for a high point of 354m to the left of the obvious trees that can be seen on the skyline. This is fine country and the views gradually open up as you gain height. If you're blessed with good weather, you'll probably want to stop at the top for a while and soak in the scene. If not, then it is pretty exposed up here and you'll probably need to get moving fairly soon.

Start off down what is actually the top of the Moneynut Valley. After a mile or so, though, the road enters a forested area and crosses the stream to head uphill. The gradient soon eases and you'll come to a junction. In fact, both roads bring you to more or less the same place on the **Cranshaws** road. If you follow the one on the right then it soon comes out of the trees and drops quite steeply down into the valley from where a few leisurely miles alongside the Whiteadder bring you back to Ellemford Bridge.

6. Coldingham

Distance:	21 miles
OS Map:	Landranger 67
Start:	Eyemouth
Grade:	3
Surface:	road 14 miles
	track 1 mile
	path 6 miles

The Berwickshire coastline is, for the most part, rugged and uncompromising. Amongst this turmoil, though, there is space for a few quiet coves and secluded beaches. You follow an inland route from Eyemouth up onto Coldingham Moor, take a loop round to Coldingham village and then go to St Abbs to pick up a coastal trail from there back to the start. There's also an option to visit Fast Castle in its curious setting overlooking the North Sea. The route will involve carrying your bike up some sets of steps, and also an uphill push for a while, so you should be prepared for that.

It's fair to say that Eyemouth doesn't win awards for its beauty but it does have some attractions. The beach has fine views to the nearby cliffs that overlook it, and the modernised harbour is full of interest. It's a fishing port and working town first, and catering for visitors seems to take a lower priority. That said, it's a friendly enough place and has the usual range of shops, pubs and so on.

Although the main east coast rail line isn't far away, the nearest station is at Berwick and access by train is therefore a bit of a chore. There is ample parking if you're travelling by car.

Take the road out of **Eyemouth** as if you're going to Coldingham, but cross straight over the main A1107 climbing gently towards Alemill. Turn left at a road junction to cross a small stream and then immediately right to climb again, this time towards Whitfield. Easier gradients lead past Press Castle and up to Coldingham Moor, where you need to join the main road for two and a half miles; not that

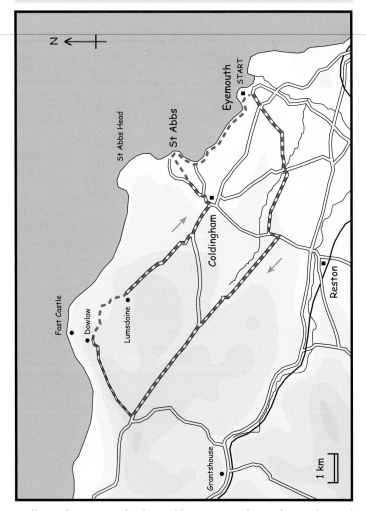

traffic up here is much of a problem. Turn right on the road signed for Fast Castle and enjoy views of the Bass Rock, North Berwick Law and Fife in the distance. Torness nuclear power station was clearly built with an eye to functionality rather than for any aesthetic appeal.

The road ends at a small parking area by **Dowlaw** farm. Access to **Fast Castle** is down a track to the left which passes a line of old farm cottages. Cycling along the path is not recommended as it soon becomes fairly exposed and drops away to the sea below. The castle is perched on a promontory some way down the cliffs and its origins date back to the early 14th century. Quite why it was built here, of all places, is a bit of a mystery.

Retrace your steps to Dowlaw. You're aiming now to reach **Lumsdaine** farm, which you'll soon be able to see to the southeast. It may not seem like it, but there is an old right of way between Dowlaw and Lumsdaine, though it doesn't get a lot of use and you might feel as if you're trespassing. You're not, but the route isn't obvious so try not to stray off it.

Pass Dowlaw farmhouse to your left and follow the track round to the left and then almost immediately turn right to aim for a gate. Go through the gate and follow the track down the edge of a field, keeping the wall and a line of telegraph poles to your right. As you go, try to pick out the line that the track takes going up through the middle of another field that you can see ahead of you.

Further down the field, the wall kinks to the right but the track leads to a line of hawthorn trees. Up ahead is some old rusting farm machinery with a gate to either side of it. The left-hand one is probably easier to use and you cross an old stone bridge – it's so overgrown that you may not even realise that it is a bridge.

Now for the hard bit, and you're going to have to push for a while. The line goes straight up through the field to reach a fence on the left and then, just a little further on, a track that leads without difficulty to Lumsdaine. Your efforts will soon be rewarded with a fine run right down to **Coldingham**, a pretty village with a shop and a couple of pubs. In summer the narrow roads can get quite busy as this is the only access road to St Abbs, another popular destination for tourists.

Take the road to **St Abbs** and enjoy the views as you roll towards the sea. Stay with the road all the way if you wish but, as an interesting alternative, a track known locally as the Creel Road starts at a layby on the right at (909 666) and leads down between hedges directly into the village to emerge by the harbour.

Of course, fishing used to be the mainstay of the local economy but that has declined in recent years. The picturesque harbour has always been a magnet for tourists, but St Abbs is now also very popular with divers and, being so small, it's a bustling place at weekends.

Just above the harbour is a row of cottages. The road in front of them leads to a path that takes you round to Coldingham Bay. When you get there, ignore the steps that lead down onto the beach but go straight on to meet the road that comes down from Coldingham. The bay has been a holiday haunt for several generations and has a timeless quality to it. There's a fine beach, and the painted wooden beach huts look just as they did fifty years ago.

Some more hard work now. Push your bike over the soft sand past the cafe and at the far end of the beach a path leads quite steeply up and over to a smaller bay with a stony beach. Steep steps lead from here up onto the cliff path that takes you down to Linkum Shore. Only the keen venture this far and you might well find that you've got the beach to yourself. In any event, this is a fine spot and you may want to have a bite to eat or simply sit and watch the sea for a while.

A grassy track leads along the shore and, just when you're wondering how to get up the cliffs ahead, the path turns right into a glen and more steps lead to a clifftop path with a bench where you can rest for a minute and catch your breath. The path is quite narrow and a little awkward in places but it does improve as you get nearer to **Eyemouth**. As the town comes into view, you have the option of going round the back of the caravan site or just taking the obvious direct route back to the start.

7. Moorfoot Hills

Distance:	**30 miles**
OS Map:	**Landranger 66**
Start:	**Gorebridge**
Grade:	**4**
Surface:	**road** **25.5 miles**
	track **1 mile**
	path **3.5 miles**

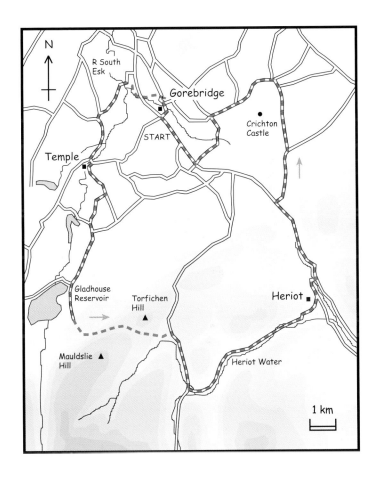

The Moorfoot Hills form a natural barrier running from northeast to southwest just a few miles south of Edinburgh. The escarpment is particularly striking at its northern edge and this route involves a strenuous uphill push to breach its defences – a sense of humour *will be an essential asset for this section. You also explore the little-known, and delightfully tranquil, Gore Glen and find time to visit Crichton Castle. A dry day and a westerly breeze would be ideal for the trip.*

There's a small cemetery and parking area on the A7 near Gorebridge at (346 604), just south of the junction with the B6372. The route is described from here.

Take the main road north for a few yards but turn off to the right for **Gorebridge** and follow the road round and downhill. Just as it starts to go uphill, look for a garage on the right with a green roof. Turn right as you reach it and aim for the back of some newish houses where the old Waverley rail line used to run. There's a path that runs behind the houses and under the old rail bridge to emerge in more open country-side with views of the Pentlands ahead of you.

After about half a mile, and as you near the A7, the trail swings to the right. Turn off left here onto a smaller path, through a gate and down a steep slope – you're aiming to go under Shank Bridge. Follow the path through some bushes, to the right at first and then straight on to come out into a more open grassy area. The River Gore is to your left and following near to its bank you head into bushes again, pass-ing a small pond. The path down the glen has undergone renovation and there are steps in places. It is a fine run through the trees and comes out by a stone bridge near the junction of the River Gore and the South Esk.

The stone bridge was apparently part of an old coaching route to Edinburgh. There's a good path going left to follow the South Esk for a while and you might want to explore a little way along here. The tran-quillity of the glen makes it difficult to believe that you're right in the middle of Midlothian and just yards from the main A7.

After a few yards the track meets a minor road by a small parking area. Turn left here and cross the bridge to head towards the village of Carrington and then take the minor road to **Temple**, a rather twee place with its red tile roofs. Quiet lanes lead to Gladhouse, and when you reach **Gladhouse Reservoir** carry on to the south for Mauldslie. By now you should have a pretty good idea of what's up ahead, but you really can't turn back now, can you?

At the T-junction Mauldslie is just along to the right, but you go through the gate and take the track heading straight on and slightly uphill to pass a clump of trees. The path now gets more indistinct – and, it must be said, sometimes wet – and you need to head for the top right corner of another clump of trees on the hillside so that you can pass round behind it.

Aim roughly northeast now towards yet another stand of trees, and in order to find the vague grassy track, you should be about 200m up the hillside from the edge of the trees as you draw level with them. This is a pretty indistinct line heading diagonally up the side of the hill and it gets even more vague as you get nearer the col. This is where your sense of humour will be sorely tested – either that, or take plenty of cash for the swear box…

Don't forget to look behind now and again – the Pentlands dominate the view to the north, and in any event you'll want to take a few minutes at the top, if only to get your breath back. The path from the col heading down to a farm access track is much better. Turn left onto the track by a barn and go along to meet the Innerleithen road with

Old rail route, Gorebridge, with the Pentland Hills in the distance

good views now of the impressive heather-covered hills and valleys to the south.

Turn right and enjoy the well-earned roll downhill towards Innerleithen. Turn left at the junction for **Heriot** and, if you've got a westerly wind, the run along the valley is a treat. You'll need to take to the A7 now for a couple of miles heading north before turning off on the B6367, signed for Pathhead and Crichton Castle. Follow the signs for Crichton, and the road to the castle takes you to a small car park from where a track leads to **Crichton Castle** itself.

Like many Scottish castles, the history of Crichton is convoluted. It began life in the 14th century as a tower and has been adapted and enlarged by its various lords and lieges as their respective fortunes rose and, more often than not, fell. It is now in the more diligent ownership of Historic Scotland. An interesting feature is the impressive and unusual Italian decorative stonework in the dining room.

There is a track marked on the map leading towards Borthwick Castle. It leads down to cross the stream behind the castle, but the track soon deteriorates and cannot really be recommended. Instead, you should retrace your steps to Crichton village and take the left turn for Gorebridge, going steeply down to cross the Tyne Water and then equally steeply up again. There's a good view of the castle from here.

Reaching a crossroads, your route turns left for North Middleton, where the Middleton Inn does snacks and drinks, and then along the A7 for a mile or so back to the start. Alternatively, if you go straight on at the crossroads and take a sharp left turn down the hill, then this would be a slightly shorter route back.

8. Lammermuirs

Distance:	**45 miles**
OS Maps:	**Landranger 66, 67, 73**
Start:	**Lauder**
Grade:	**5**
Surface:	**road 27 miles**
	track 7 miles
	path 11 miles

The Lammermuir Hills sit proudly to the southeast of Edinburgh and the rolling heather-covered summits rise to a maximum height of just over 500m at Lammer Law. This route takes you to within a few hundred yards of that summit. The complete circuit has significant height gain and loss, added to which it crosses some isolated moorland and, as such, should be considered as a fairly arduous trip. Having said that, though, if you get some good weather then there's no doubt that it'll be a day to remember.

The Southern Upland Way passes through **Lauder** and, indeed, you'll be cycling part of it on this route. The parish church in the town is quite unusual in that it's laid out in the shape of a cross with the pulpit in the

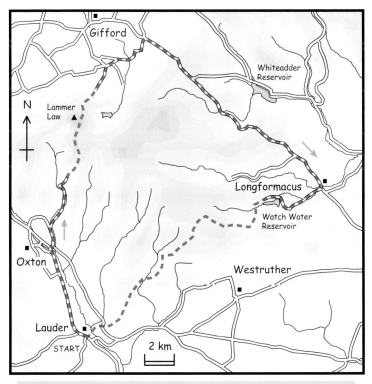

centre, under the bell tower. There are plenty of shops but none on the route, so take with you all that you need.

Unfortunately, there's little alternative but to cycle four miles along the A68 to Carfraemill. For part of the way there is the dubious 'protection' of a solid white line on the road, but it really isn't ideal. If it's possible to arrange transport to avoid using the main road then that might be a good idea.

From Carfraemill, then, cycle up the valley towards Tollishill. After three miles there's a sharp right turn and the road heads steeply uphill in no uncertain manner. The gradient only eases as you reach a gate by a stand of trees…but don't relax, because there's more to come yet.

This is an old right of way across the hills and runs between Haddington and Lauder. A number of tracks lead off from it and you may wish to explore them. The Scottish Outdoor Access Code allows freer access than used to be the case in this area, although caution is advised in the shooting season. In any event, as the trail climbs higher the hills and valleys roll away in all directions and you can't fail to be moved by the grandeur of the area.

A high point of over 500m is reached just to the east of **Lammer Law** summit, so you can relax for a while as the track drops 300m in three miles to reach the farm at Longyester. If you feel the urge to make a detour into **Gifford** where there are shops and a couple of pubs then turn left here. It will add extra mileage to the journey, though, and also an extra hill to climb. The main route turns right and works its way round quiet lanes to join the B6355 at a crossroads with a rather quaint direction indicator.

From arable farmland, the route soon makes the transition back to open moorland as the road climbs, gently at first, but then fairly relentlessly to over 400m. There's a junction and you take the right fork, signposted for Longformacus (pronounced 'long for make us'). The road dips and climbs for several miles now, weaving through the hills, and you'll get glimpses of the sea over to the east. Enjoy the roll down into the village, but **Longformacus** itself is little more than just a few houses so don't expect much in the way of facilities – I can recall on one occasion, however, having lunch in the bus shelter; it being the only haven from the non-stop rain!

From here, take the road for **Watch Water Reservoir** and brace yourself for a fairly steep haul for a mile or so. The surfaced road continues to Scarlaw farm, and the rest of the route back to Lauder follows the Southern Upland Way on tracks and paths. If there has been a spell of wet weather then this section could be fairly hard work.

Ahead you can see the obvious cairns that mark the hill called Twin Law Cairns and it's there that you aim for next. A track continues straight on past the farm for a short way before a sign points you to the left on another track heading south. It crosses a stream then climbs gently to a col by a fence. A grassy path leads off to the right and up towards the summit but there's a bit of work involved in getting to it. There is a tale that a Scots and English army each sent a champion to single combat. They fought to the death, each unaware that the other was his brother, and the cairns were erected in memory of them both. Whether true or not, it's certainly the stuff of legend…

There have been some changes to the Southern Upland Way over the years and it has been re-routed in places, so might not correspond exactly with your map. There are some ups and downs to come but eventually you'll emerge on the main A697 road. The route continues across the road and drops down into the grounds of Thirlstane Castle. The castle, with its distinctive and unusual turrets, dates to the 16th century and was the ancestral seat of the Earls and Duke of Lauderdale, whose ghost is said to haunt it.

Ghosts or not, from here it's just a short way up into the town centre and you might wish to raise a glass to what has surely been a fine day out.

9. Norham

Distance:	31 miles
OS Map:	Landranger 74
Start:	Duns
Grade:	2
Surface:	road 31 miles

A fairly leisurely jaunt, all on road and with no serious gradients, exploring the country between Duns and the River Tweed. The route starts from Duns, the county town of Berwickshire with a busy town centre. Nearby is the Duns Castle Country Park, while the town itself has the Jim Clark Room in memory of the local, and famous, motor racing driver.

From **Duns** take the main road for Chirnside and Berwick out of the town, but only for a short way before turning off to the right for Wedderburn. Several routes are possible; yours takes a left turn to pass Turtleton and cross Blackadder Water by a rather fine bridge – originally built in 1795 – and called The Mouth.

The area here, between the Tweed and the Lammermuirs, is known as the Merse. It's undulating countryside, and the patchwork of roads, with their rectilinear evolution, probably reflects patterns of land ownership.

Whitsome is on a small, but prominent hill and is little more than a few cottages clustered around a small church and cemetery. This tranquil rural setting belies a rich, and sometimes turbulent, history which goes back a long way – relics of Roman occupation have been found nearby. In 1482 the village was burnt to the ground by the Duke of Gloucester, who was later to become Richard III of England. Despite this, though, Whitsome was a thriving community of several hundred, even at the turn of the 20th century.

Approaching Norham, you'll see the outline of Ladykirk Church over to the left just before you go steeply downhill to cross the Tweed into England. **Norham** village is just a little further on and comes complete with village green, a couple of pubs and tidy rows of cottages. The impressive Norham Castle, high up on the hill above the Tweed, looks down over the scene.

Take the road that leads up past the **castle** and follow it round to **Horncliffe**. The route doesn't actually go into Horncliffe since there's no through road. It is a pleasant village, though, and you may have time to take a look along the main street. The village stands well above the Tweed and there are paths leading down to it which could be worth exploring. If you turn right at the pub you'll see a sign on the left after 50 yards or so pointing to a footpath down to the river.

Leave the village by the same road that you came into it and turn left to head towards the Union Bridge, a narrow suspension bridge crossing the Tweed. Before the A1 bypass was built, this was the next bridge upriver from the Royal Border Bridge in Berwick and one of only a handful spanning the Tweed between Kelso and the coast.

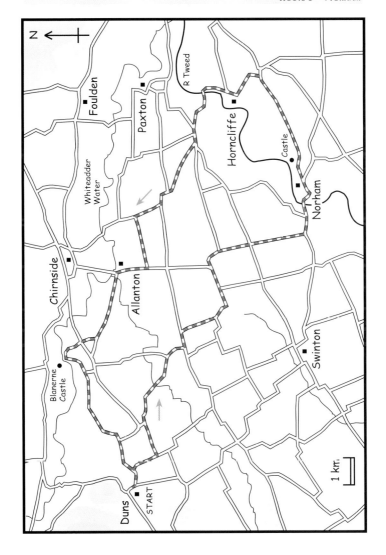

Norham Castle

Follow the lanes to **Allanton**, another small village with an inn, and turn left to cross Blackadder Water for a second time. Turn right just past Whitemire. This is closed to cars, but you can cycle past the weighbridge to meet the main road. Taking the back road round by Todheugh should give you a glimpse of the **Blanerne Castle** ruins across the river.

There's no avoiding the steady, but gentle, climb now up towards Buxley, the towers and turrets of which are quite impressive over to the left. Manderston House, a little further on, is Edwardian and was lavishly constructed. It is not easily seen from the road but it is open to the public and boasts the only silver staircase in the world.

When you reach the main road there's a mile or so of easy cycling back into **Duns**.

10. Merse

Distance:	33 miles
OS Map:	Landranger 74
Start:	Greenlaw
Grade:	2
Surface:	road 30.5 miles/34 miles
	track 2.5 miles

The relatively flat land between the Tweed and the Lammermuir Hills to the north is called the Merse. There doesn't seem to be a strict definition of this term, nor will you find any boundaries, so we'll just take a relaxed view and use it loosely. In all honesty, the area can't be described as having a dramatic landscape but, strangely enough, this route is actually a good one to do in the rain. There's something therapeutic about cycling in the wet. Maybe it's to do with the dank rural smells, or maybe it's simply because you feel more virtuous having made the effort to get out and actually do something. Of course, it's a nice route to do when it's sunny, too...

Greenlaw used to be the county town of Berwickshire, but nowadays the place seems to lack any focus and doesn't have an awful lot to offer the visitor. The old courthouse is a prominent building, but it has fallen into disuse and has been boarded up for some years. There are shops and a hotel or two, however, and the route starts here.

Take the main A6105 for Earlston, but only for half a mile or so before turning off to the left towards **Hume Castle**. The castle is perched on a high point giving views over the surrounding countryside. Like others, it has been fought over, demolished, rebuilt and fought over again.

From Hume Castle there are several routes which take you to **Eccles** and the remains of St Mary's Convent. Quite why the village has a white post box, instead of the normal red, is a bit of a mystery but no doubt there's a sound reason.

The road past Fernyrig Cottage and Birgham Wood brings you to

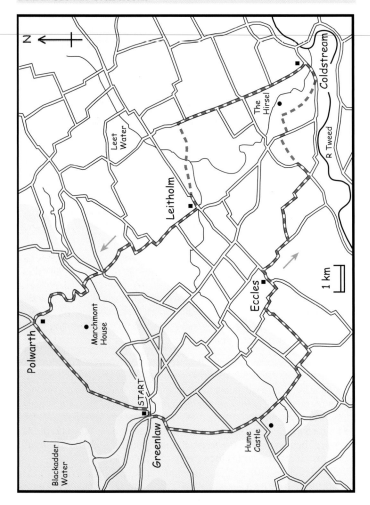

the main Kelso to Coldstream road, but you turn left almost immediately towards Haigsfield. At Haigsfield the road takes a sharp left turn but you can follow the track straight on to come out on the A697. Take the main road towards Coldstream for about 400 yards then turn left into the Hirsel Estate.

Avoid this by following the minor road to come out on the A697 a little further to the north.

The Hirsel was owned by the former Prime Minister, Alec Douglas Home. Hirsel House is not open to the public but the estate grounds are; there are tea rooms and craft shops. Follow the estate road and take a right fork where you see a large gabled building to the left. You'll pass a lake, golf course and craft centre to emerge again on the road into **Coldstream**.

The town, which gives its name to the Guards regiment, has plenty of facilities. There is also a museum, and you might want to take a look at the Marjoribanks Monument and the elegant bridge over the Tweed which marks the border with England. When the Stone of Destiny was returned to Scotland after an absence of 700 years this was the place chosen for it to be brought across the border on what was a rather poignant ceremonial occasion.

Our route takes a left turn on the main street along Guards Road and heads northwesterly in pretty much a straight line for several miles. This is gently undulating country and eventually you're looking for a track to Marlfield. The track aims for Leitholm and crosses Leet Water by a footbridge. In really wet weather – and you may just be lucky – actually getting to the bridge can be a little problematic and you might simply have to settle for wet feet.

Staying with the road instead of the track will add about three-quarters of a mile to the total distance.

Leitholm is a small village and you'll take a right turn at the end of the main street, again heading northwest. Eventually this meets the B6460 road and here you have a choice. If time is short then you can aim directly back to Greenlaw and cut corresponding distance off the journey. The next part of the route, though quite hilly, does have much of interest, however, and is included for that reason.

Go straight across at the crossroads, drop down a little to cross Blackadder Water then go past Sisterpath. The road goes quite steeply down to cross a small burn at the site of what was Marchmont Station on a now disused rail route. It continues up to the right alongside banks which are covered in primroses in the Spring. At the top of this hill stop and look to your left along a beech avenue to the impressive facade of **Marchmont House**, a mile or so away. To your right the avenue continues to an old dovecot, the building you can see at the end of it. Curiously, the avenue was never actually used as a main access to the house but was really designed as a cosmetic exercise.

Turn the next bend and you can't fail to notice the imposing outline of **Polwarth** church perched on the skyline. Polworth used to be a thriving community of 200 or so people, most of whom were involved in tanning, but there are now just a few scattered cottages remaining.

Although it is a main road, the traffic here isn't usually a problem. There is a little more work to do, however, and it's about three miles back to **Greenlaw**. For much of that you'll have woodland on your left and open moorland to the right before rolling downhill into the town.

11. Lindisfarne

Distance:	**27 miles**
OS Map:	**Landranger 75**
Start:	**Spittal**
Grade:	**2**
Surface:	**road 18 miles**
	track 7 miles
	path 2 miles

A coastal route on tracks and bridleways that crosses the causeway to Holy Island, or Lindisfarne. Since the causeway is under water at high tide you will need to check beforehand and make sure that you've got enough time to get on and off the island. The Tourist Information Office in Berwick will be able to tell you when the road is open.

The walled town of Berwick at the mouth of the Tweed has had a more turbulent history than most and it has, in fact, changed hands between Scotland and England a dozen or more times. A good view of the town, and of the Royal Border Bridge which spans the Tweed, can be had from the south bank of the river near where this route starts.

At the mouth of the river, and opposite the pier in Berwick, is a small car park out on the point at (005 521). From here it's just a couple

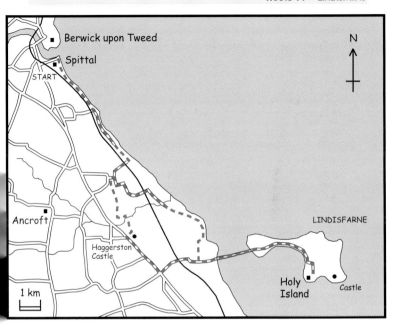

of minutes to the promenade at **Spittal**, and if you follow this along as far as the last house, you'll find a surfaced track on the right. This takes you up onto the low cliffs and gives good views back to Berwick. To the south you can pick out Lindisfarne and to its right the outline of Bamburgh Castle.

The grassy track continues for a couple of miles to join a road at Sea House which runs parallel to the beach. A mile or so down here brings you to a small car park by an old wartime pill box. Take the track round to the right of this and go through a gate into the nature reserve. Sand dunes are on your left as the track heads southeast and past a small lake. Stop at a 'crossroads' by a bridge over the railway after a mile.

Because there is a golf course further on it is recommended that you skirt it to avoid any potential problems. It might be possible to head onto the beach and either push for a while or, depending on the tide, find firm sand to cycle on. If that doesn't appeal then you need to cross the bridge and head slightly uphill to Cheswick. When you get there take the left turn which brings you on the road running down to the golf course clubhouse.

A mile further on is Goswick farm. The route continues past a caravan site and follows a path which hugs the coastline and gives fine views of the now familiar outline of Holy Island. Follow the track round to cross a small bridge before aiming south to join the Holy Island access road near Beal.

From here it's just a short way along the road to the causeway. When you get to the start of the causeway there's a small parking area and a notice listing the safe crossing times – ignore this at your peril!

If the weather is on your side then it's easy to spend some time on **Lindisfarne**. The first monastery was founded by St Aidan in about 635 AD while work on the priory started in 1093. There's also the castle, shops, pubs and the north of the island is a haven for wildlife. Try some of the Holy Island mead...but keep an eye on the tide if you do!

While it's certainly possible to retrace the same route there is an inland diversion for the return journey or, at least, part of it. It goes via Haggerston Castle and some bridleways. Make sure you have a decent map because these trails aren't used very much and the route isn't always obvious. That, however, is one of its attractions in my view, and it's also an opportunity to do what you can to make sure that they don't fall into disuse.

Take the main road off the island and carry on to where it meets the main A1 at the Plough Inn. There really isn't much choice here but to cycle on the main road for a mile and a bit to **Haggerston Castle**. Although quite a fine building, the castle and grounds have been developed as a sort of 'fun park' for children. Incidentally, what looks on the map like a possible route alongside the railway line and into the 'back' of the castle doesn't go – padlocked gates etc.

So, go past the main entrance to the castle – unless you want to go in, that is – and take the 'Picnic Area' turning. There's a phone box and although a sign says 'residents only' this is, in fact, a public bridleway so go ahead. Turn left just as you come to a high red brick wall. A few yards along here, as you pass some cottages on the left, go straight ahead looking for a small gate with a blue 'bridleway' sign on it. Go through this, and a couple of others, and follow the right edge of a field. At the far end there's another gate that brings you out by a cattle grid.

Look ahead and diagonally over to your left to spot the next gate. The route goes along the left edge of a field now, aiming for a small stone bridge. Cross the bridge, go sharp right then sharp left, following a track that leads past a wind pump and up towards some farm buildings. As you reach the buildings take the track to pass the cottages on your right. This enters a field following the left side to continue into yet another field. When I was there, this second field had recently been ploughed and sown, but the route actually goes straight across the middle of it, through a hedgerow, and straight across the middle of the next field as well to reach a gate with the familiar 'bridleway' sign. Looking ahead you'll see the obvious Ladythorne House – the route passes in front of this and goes up to join the road. Turn right and then left to join the outward route.

12. St Cuthbert's Cave

Distance:	**26 miles**
OS Map:	**Landranger 75**
Start:	**Ford**
Grade:	**3**
Surface:	**road 16 miles**
	track 6 miles
	path 4 miles

Meandering around parts of north Northumberland, this is not so much a circular route but more a figure-of-eight. It just seemed to evolve that way but, in doing so, it does create a number of options as to how you might tackle it.

Ford is a model village and unnervingly neat and tidy, so you really should take a look around – spot, for example, the front door built in the shape of a horseshoe. The elegant Ford Castle is where James IV of Scotland spent his last night before falling victim to the slaughter at nearby Flodden. The equally elegant Lady Waterford Gallery in the village, a former schoolhouse, has an unusual display of biblical murals.

Approaching Ford from the west, you'll cross the River Till by a stone bridge. If you start from here, then turn right to go along and then swing left up the hill towards the village. Take a right turn for Kimmerston, but just a short way down here turn left onto the farm track for Ford Hill. Pass the farm buildings and carry on to meet a surfaced road at the corner of a wood. Turn right then left to go up to **Ford Moss**.

You can see evidence of an industry long since gone. The remains of the chimney show where there was a steam engine that pumped water from the colliery. The site of the colliery village is just nearby, but there is little to be seen of it now and the area is designated a nature reserve.

Follow the bridleway up the hill, to the right of some trees. Fine views are revealed as you near the top of the moor – the Cheviots are close by but you can also catch the familiar outline of the Eildons to the west. The North Sea is visible to the east. The track leads downwards now passing below Goats Crag, one of several sandstone outcrops in the area, and then on to Routin Lynn farm. Follow the farm track to the edge of a wood where it veers to the right, joining the surfaced road after a few hundred yards at a T-junction.

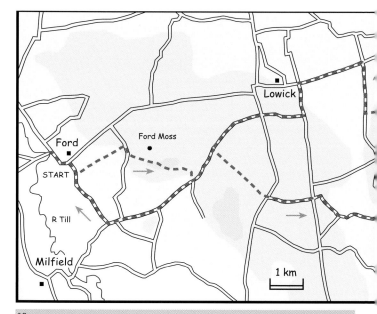

Turn left, but after a hundred yards look for a sign pointing down a path on the left. This is a good example of an ancient 'cup and ring-marked stone'. The significance of these markings, and others like them, is not clear, but it's only a couple of hundred yards away and so you might wish to take the short detour to see for yourself.

Shortly over half a mile brings you to a wooden post with a sign for a bridleway to the right. This is the 'direct route', but I'd have to say that it can be harder going than it appears from the road and a little frustrating in places, particularly in wet conditions. It's the way to go if you're feeling up to it, but there is an easier option – if a little longer – round by the road. The bridleway traverses fairly featureless pastureland for over a mile to bring you out at another junction.

This section can be avoided if you carry on along the road to meet the B6525 and turn right to pass Barmoor Red House. It will add a mile and a half to the total distance.

Work your way east along the lanes to Hutton North Farm, Hutton Steads and on to Holburn Grange. You can see the ridge ahead and

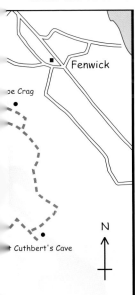

St Cuthbert's Cave is hidden in the trees near their left edge. In fact, you're following part of St Cuthbert's Way, a long-distance footpath that takes the route supposedly followed by St Cuthbert when he travelled from Melrose to the monastery at Lindisfarne.

From the small car parking area, a track leads uphill for a few hundred yards before turning sharp right to contour along the hillside. At the corner of the woods you'll see that St Cuthbert's Way, and your route, takes the track up the hill. To see the cave, though, go straight on for a few yards, then follow the obvious trail on the left up into the trees.

Retrace your steps to the corner of the woods and make your way uphill along the edge of the trees. Crest the grassy ridge and Lindisfarne, or Holy Island, is set out before you, much as it would have been to St Cuthbert at this same spot back in the 7th century. The scene changes with the tides, the seasons and

Ford Castle

the weather, but is always one to demand more than just a passing glance.

Still following St Cuthbert's Way, the grassy track heads down the slope to join a farm track. Turn left onto it, towards some woods. Just after entering the trees, take a right turn and go round as the track swings right and then left in front of a large stone house. Just a few yards further on and a sign points you down a narrow trail on the right which can be a little boggy at times. There are a couple of small bridges over streams – stop at a 'crossroads' beyond the last of these at (061 377).

St Cuthbert's Way goes straight on here but you go left into the wood. After half a mile the track bends to the right and you take a turn to the left at (054 384). There should be a small wooden hut to your left, just by a fork in the track. The right fork takes you towards **Kyloe Crag**, which can be glimpsed through the trees if you go that way, while the left fork takes you past a crag known as 'Kyloe in the Wood' and some curiously shaped rock formations almost hidden in the forest on your right. You can use either route, but perhaps the left fork is easier to navigate as it follows a generally westwards direction and cruises down to meet the road at a gate (035 390).

Cycle easily into **Lowick** where you can find a couple of shops and pubs. Take a left turn half way along the main street. This road follows the course of the Roman road called 'Devils' Causeway' but you turn off to the right after half a mile. It's just a case now of ambling along the lanes, and making sure that you don't miss the right turn for Kimmerston and **Ford**.

13. Tweedsmuir

Distance:	55 miles
OS Maps:	Landranger 72, 73
Start:	Gordon Arms Hotel, Yarrow Valley
Grade:	5
Surface:	road 55 miles

This is the longest route in the book, though it's possible to shave off three or four miles using the optional detours, one of which involves wading the Tweed. You travel through some of the finest that the Southern Uplands has to offer and take in what must be one of the steepest climbs in southern Scotland to reach a high point of 450m at the Megget Stone. In winter, and if there's been recent snow, you may want to check that this road is actually open before committing yourself.

The route is described from the Yarrow Valley but there's no reason why you couldn't start from Peebles or wherever suits you.

Take the road up for Traquair and Innerleithen crossing the watershed to roll down into the Tweed Valley. Turn left at Traquair to pass Traquair House, said to be the oldest inhabited house in

Scotland. You'll also pass the Bear Gates, locked by the Fifth Earl of Traquair in 1745 as Bonnie Prince Charlie left, with a promise that they would only be unlocked when there was another Stuart on the throne. They have, of course, remained closed ever since. The house contains numerous historical treasures and is worth a visit in its own right. It also boasts a small brewery and there are several craft workshops in the grounds. If you want to call in then don't turn left at Traquair; the entrance is a few hundred yards down the road towards **Innerleithen**.

A few miles further, on the way to Peebles, you'll pass Kailzie Gardens. The gardens are open to the public and there's a restaurant/ tearoom. Further still, and the road enters **Peebles** along the south bank of the Tweed by a car park and grassy area that's often used for picnics. The bustling town centre is on the other side of the river, and you can use either the old stone road bridge or the pedestrian suspension bridge at the east end of the car park.

At this stage you need to consider which route to take out of the town. Two are described here, leaving you to decide. There is the main A72 road and there is the quieter, but longer, alternative round to the south, but using minor roads. I'll mention, in passing, that between these two lies a third option. Since it involves a fairly brutal ascent over Manor Sware and an even steeper descent, it really wouldn't be my favoured choice. It does, however, offer a fine viewpoint as compensation for the pain involved in getting there.

To find my preferred route, go to the west end of the car park by the Tweed and look over the street to locate Springhill Road. Follow it, heading gently uphill and round to the right. You need to turn right up Springwood Road and then almost immediately left along Bonnington Road. You're following signs for Cademuir and this is also part of the Tweed Cycleway. The road climbs a little more, but you're soon out into open country with superb views of the hills to the south, and the gradient here gives a pleasant run right around the foot of Cademuir Hill.

Cross the Manor Water by a narrow stone bridge and climb to a T-junction at the Glack. The road to the right is a dead-end and climbs a little further, as far as Caverhill. Roll down to Haswellsykes and then turn right and down again to a cottage by the Tweed. A path leads through the trees to the left and along the bank to a footbridge. The route up to Lyne Station is clear and you go under the old rail bridge that spans

Goats Crag near Ford (Route 12)

Smailholm Tower (Route 17)

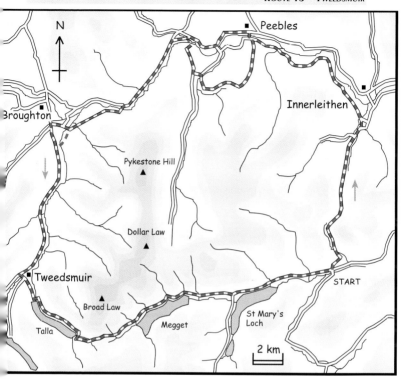

both the road and the river to join a minor road which cuts between the A72 and the B712. Turn left to head for the B712 **Broughton** road.

By far the shortest and easiest way is to follow the A72 for three miles out of Peebles before taking a left turn towards what was Lyne Station on the old railway. This will lead shortly to the B712 Broughton road. This route also offers fine views of Neidpath Castle, perched high above the Tweed and the location for a number of film sets. It is, however, a main road and you might prefer the more peaceful alternative.

Using the main road, as described above, will reduce the trip distance by three miles.

Joining the B712, then, you'll pass Stobo Castle and also the Botanic Gardens at Dawyck – home to an unusual collection of trees including, it is said, the unique Dawyck Beech. Just after Drumelzier the road takes a sharp right turn to join the main A701 at Rachan Mill.

It is possible to cut another mile off the journey by going straight on at the bend, down the track past Drumelzier Place and fording the Tweed. It is quite wide here and, therefore, normally quite shallow. Take your shoes off and you'll simply get wet feet. Follow the track on the opposite bank up to the main road.

It's quite a haul along the A701 to Tweedsmuir. There may be a route along the other side of the valley – parts of it certainly exist, but whether it's unbroken or not is another matter; I rather doubt it. A mile or two before Tweedsmuir is the old Crook Inn which dates back over 400 years. Sadly it closed some time ago and its future is currently uncertain.

Tweedsmuir is just a small village – one church, no pub, no shop – just off the main road. The school was closed years ago, but until relatively recently it was run by the local education authority as an outdoor centre catering for small groups in this most tranquil of areas. Budget cuts forced its sale, though, and the centre is now privately managed.

The road through the village is signposted for **Talla** Reservoir, built to serve the needs of Edinburgh. A mile or so brings you to the reservoir; a fine sight in this steep-sided valley. It's not really until you're some way down it that you realise that the way out of this is up The Hill, and at 15% it is a fierce haul indeed! No excuses, though; get your head down, put something soothing on the walkman, and just embrace the inevitable. As you climb, the views unfold and, whatever the mood and the weather, this is surely a fine place to be. Stop at the bridge over the stream to take it all in – there's a little more uphill to come, but you've done all the hard work now.

Moving on, the Megget Stone is right by the cattle grid and marks the watershed. The hills around here are really quite stunning and make tremendous ski touring country in the right conditions. Sometimes, even when the road is clear and many of the slopes bare, there's a ribbon of snow in a stream bed just a short way along from the Megget Stone which comes right down to the road and so gives access by ski to the slopes up onto Broad Law, the highest point in southern Scotland.

Enjoy the roll down to the **Megget** Reservoir and down even further to **St Mary's Loch** in the Yarrow Valley. It's easy to see the attraction of the place as the steep-sided hills tumble straight down to the water's edge. From here it's a leisurely four or five miles along to the Gordon Arms where, if you've used the car park, you might think it polite to give them some of your custom in return – in any event, you'll have earned a break at the end of this route!

14. Minch Moor

Distance:	22 miles	
OS Map:	Landranger 73	
Start:	Yair Bridge, Selkirk	
Grade:	3	
Surface:	road	9 miles
	track	4 miles
	path	9 miles

A classic route following an old drove road as it picks its way along an undulating ridge and climbs to over 500m. Choose a clear day and you'll be rewarded with spectacular views. The area, in general, has a lot to offer in terms of off-road trails and the Tweed Valley is a justifiably popular area with riders coming from far and wide to enjoy the purpose-built trails in Glentress and Elibank forests.

Our route starts from **Yair Bridge** where it spans the Tweed just north of Selkirk. If you're arriving by car, then there's a small parking area on the south bank of the river, just a few yards to the east of the bridge.

Take the road following the south bank of the Tweed. This is part of NCR1 and soon turns into a track as it leads round towards the site of the former Peel Hospital. We've joined a minor road as it trends upwards along the south side of the Tweed Valley. The hills and sides of the valley dominate the scene as you work your way along. Elibank Castle in the trees up on the left dates back over 400 years, though it was abandoned in the late 17th century and left to fall into the state that you see it now.

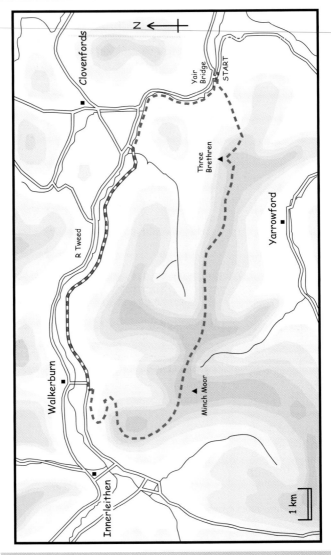

Ignore the right turn for **Walkerburn** but shortly after it, look for the start of a forest track on the left at (358 367). The trail gains height and at the first major junction take the left turn. At the next junction turn right and you'll still be climbing for most of the way until it meets the Southern Upland Way coming from Traquair. Climb steeply up through the trees now – you'll probably be pushing here – and stick to the obvious track as it heads east. It's quite fierce but the gradient soon eases as you come out of the trees onto the open hillside.

Soon you'll pass the Cheese Well where, legend has it, you should leave an offering for the fairies. The path passes near to, but not over, the summit of **Minch Moor**, and you might want to take a few minutes to stroll across the heather to take in the views from the trig point. It is, quite simply, a fine place to be.

The path rises and dips with the ridge. Ignore trails off to the right. The Minchmoor Road itself heads down to Yarrowford, and later on there's a track signed for Broadmeadows Youth Hostel, again off to the right. You're aiming for the **Three Brethren**, three prominent cairns by a trig point. The cairns mark the boundaries of three of the old estates – Yair, Buccleuch and Selkirk Burgh.

From the cairns there are a couple of routes down. Yours follows the Southern Upland Way and heads southeast at first, then kinks left into the trees. It's a good path, but quite steep in places. If you take your time and are quiet enough then you could well come across deer or other wildlife on the way down. I was surprised once to round a bend and find a fox in the middle of the path just 10 yards away. We looked at each other for a moment or two before going our separate ways.

If you wanted a longer day out then you could link this with the Yair Bridge route which continues along the Southern Upland Way over the hill from Yair Bridge to Galashiels.

15. Yair Bridge

Distance:	**10 miles**
OS Map:	**Landranger 73**
Start:	**Galashiels**
Grade:	**3**
Surface:	**road 5 miles**
	track 2.5 miles
	path 2.5 miles

A short but quite demanding route. The hard work is more than adequately rewarded by the superb setting and views from the high point at over 300m. For a longer, and quite seriously demanding, day you could link this with the Minch Moor route.

As this part of the country goes Galashiels is quite a cosmopolitan place, and there's no shortage of shops, pubs and other facilities. There is no rail access, however, though there's an active campaign to reopen the old Waverley line between Carlisle and Edinburgh, or at least the section north from Galashiels. In fact, the old rail line is now a cycle route and is known locally as the 'Black Path' because of its tarred surface. The cycleway runs from just northeast of the town centre right through the middle – but with one short detour – and then for about five miles or so to just beyond Melrose.

You need to locate the Black Path because it's that route that we take out of the town. It passes under the A7 at (490 366) by the obvious brickwork that holds up the banking at that point. It follows along the base of the brick wall as far as the Abbotsford Hotel where there's a detour along the road behind the hotel and past a small roundabout. This is Currie Road and there's a car park along here past the Health Centre and large supermarket along the road at (496 360). You can pick up the cycle route again as it runs alongside the river through the trees.

After about a mile there are some playing fields before the track crosses a minor road. Turn right here to follow the road downhill to a roundabout almost underneath the prominent road bridge over the

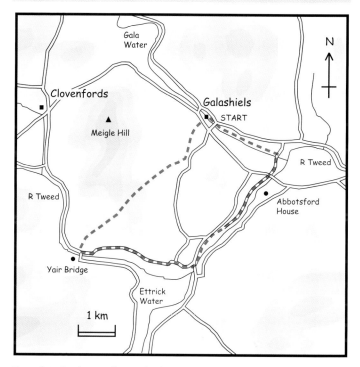

Tweed. Take the road – marked as a dead end – along the river. At this point it's actually part of the Tweed Cycle Route and also NCR1.

Look out for glimpses of the impressive architecture of **Abbotsford House** through the trees and across the river. This was Sir Walter Scott's home and is open to the public, although you'd need to make a detour if you wanted to visit. Moving on, there's a picnic area on the left, and where the road comes to an end the cycle route continues up to the A7.

The cycle route runs alongside the main road before passing underneath the bridge over the Tweed near its junction with **Ettrick Water**. When you cross the 'old brig' turn left and the route heads gently uphill from here with the Tweed down to your left. Stay with the Tweed Cycle Route as it skirts the hillside before dropping down to the river again at **Yair Bridge**.

The route over the hill back to Galashiels is actually part of the Southern Upland Way. From Yair Bridge it takes the waymarked track through Fairnilee farm. It gets fairly steep, but is rideable right up to where it comes out of trees onto open hillside, with the cottage of Calfshaw down to the right. The section from here up the steep grassy slope and through the gate is clearly one to push, but it is quite short.

Follow alongside the wall to go through another gate. The Eildons are clearly visible from here over to the east. Look for a marker post ahead and slightly to the left on the skyline. When you reach the marker post there's an optional detour up to the summit of this hill in some trees up to the right. You could leave your bike or take it with you part of the way at least. The clump of trees at the top is quite striking and the views from the top make it all worth the effort. Ruberslaw, Black Hill, the Three Brethren and the Cheviots are all prominent landmarks and can all be seen from here. It's a nice spot to stop and mull over… well, whatever needs mulling over.

Rejoin the grassy path as it heads downwards. There are several stiles to cross on the way. The Southern Upland Way used to join the Hollybush Road just where it reaches the forested area, and it's certainly possible to do that if you cross another stile and go just a few yards up the track beside the stone wall. The road leads quickly downhill to the town.

The 'official' path has now been re-routed, though, and leads over to the left and down through a wooded area called the 'Policies' to come out by the swimming pool. From there it's just a short way back to your start point.

16. Scott's View

Distance:	**29 miles**
OS Maps:	**Landranger 73**
Start:	**Melrose**
Grade:	**3**
Surface:	**road 27.5 miles**
	track 1.5 miles

The Eildon Hills are a distinctive and prominent landmark in southeast Scotland and are easily recognisable for many miles around. This tour circumnavigates them and takes in a number of towns, villages and other features on the way. It is all on road or well-surfaced cycle tracks and there are a couple of pretty steep sections to hold your attention.

Melrose sits at the foot of the Eildons and is a busy market town. Melrose Abbey was originally built some miles away near Scott's View around the middle of the 7th century, but, along with Dryburgh and Newbattle Abbey, was burnt down in 1385 on the orders of Richard II. A new abbey was built and it is the remains of this that you see now. It's a major tourist attraction, and the heart of Robert the Bruce is said to be buried in a small casket within the grounds.

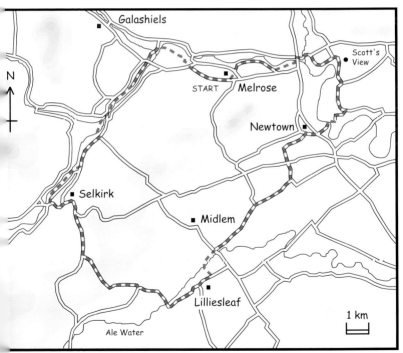

The town itself contains much of interest, and you might want to explore a little and perhaps take a look at the suspension bridge – known locally as the 'chain bridge' – which spans the Tweed to link Melrose and Gattonside, at least for pedestrians. Just upstream from the bridge is the Cauld and there's a small picnic area here. The route is described from the market square in the middle of **Melrose**.

Take the road which goes past the entrance to the abbey and follow it round to the right heading towards Newstead. (If you turn left where the road bends to the right, then you'll come to the chain bridge.) Newstead claims to be one of the oldest inhabited villages in Scotland, and who are we to doubt it? Climb up through the main street and turn left at the top of the hill, following signs for the Tweed Cycleway.

This road is barred to traffic and, as you cycle along it, you're actually crossing the site of an old Roman fort named Trimontium, after the three Eildon hills in whose shadow it lay. The site was a large one and included an amphitheatre perched high above the Tweed. There's a wooden viewing platform on the left, though it has to be said that there really isn't much to see in the way of remains and you'd need to exercise your imagination. The Ormiston Institute in the market square in Melrose has an exhibition with maps and details of how the site might have looked.

Leaderfoot Viaduct is a stunning example of Victorian engineering and carried the railway soaring over the Tweed on its way north to Earlston. The 'new' road bridge behind it is functional, but far less elegant, and the old road bridge sits down below in the shadow of its replacement.

Go over the old bridge, cycle downhill to cross Leader Water and brace yourself for a long, steep haul up to Scott's View. Some way up the hill from the Leader, just past a left turn for Redpath, take the road to the right, where you'll get a brief respite before another steep climb. By the time you reach **Scott's View**, you'll probably welcome the chance to sit down and admire it. Walter Scott lived at Abbotsford, near Melrose, and was well known for his passion for the Borders. Here, with the sweeping bend of the Tweed down below and the Eildons dominating the scene, it's easy to see how that passion could be inspired. Scott was buried at Dryburgh Abbey, which is a little further along the route.

Roll downhill and then head up to a T-junction. Turn right and you'll shortly pass Bemersyde House. This is the family home of the

Leaderfoot Viaduct over the River Tweed, near Melrose

descendants of Earl Haig – General Haig of First World War fame. Haig, of course, was a controversial proponent of that form of trench warfare which resulted in the slaughter of so many. The tranquillity of the gardens, which are open to the public, is in marked contrast to that of the Somme all those years ago.

William Wallace was a national figure of a different kind. You'll see a sign for Wallace's statue just a short way past Bemersyde House. A path leads through the woods, and the massive sandstone statue is perched at the top of a steep slope and shows Wallace, the 'Ill Requited Chief', gazing across towards the Eildons.

Moving on, there's a hill which will test your brakes and a T-junction at the bottom to ensure that every last millimetre possible is worn off them. Turn right here and another steep descent leads to a junction by a phone box. Our route takes the road to the right. Straight ahead is the driveway leading to the rather luxurious Dryburgh Abbey Hotel and to the left is the entrance to Dryburgh Abbey itself. The ruins are open to the public but there is an admission charge.

The road heads down to follow the Tweed upstream to the suspension footbridge. Notice the curious building up to the right on a mound.

This is the Temple of the Muses, built by the 11th Earl of Buchan and dedicated to local poet, James Thomson. Cross the bridge and join the road which leads to the Newtown St Boswells bypass.

If you want to cut the trip short then there is a designated cycle route which leads directly back to Melrose. Go through the town and past the obvious Scottish Borders Council offices. The route is signposted to the left, a few hundred yards further on, and it's actually part of the National Cycle Network's route number 1.

Take the road straight across the bypass that leads towards the town. It rises a little, then drops downhill. At the bottom of the dip, look out for a left turn signed for Whitelee. The road passes under an old rail bridge and climbs at first, but the gradient soon eases, and you've got a few miles now of gentle cycling through the quiet lanes which dissect this rural landscape.

You're aiming for Lilliesleaf, and about a mile before reaching it you'll arrive at Toftbarns bridge, which crosses Ale Water. Turn left and stay with the road if you wish, but it's easier, and just slightly shorter, to go straight on and bear left down a track after half a mile to cross the river at a ford. If the river is too deep then there is a footbridge a few yards downstream. There's a small grassy picnic area here, and an obvious track leads along towards the village.

On the main street through **Lilliesleaf** you'll find a Post Office and a couple of pubs. Take the right turn at the end of the street, and after a mile or so you'll re-cross Ale Water. Some hard work now for the next two miles or more as the route climbs to Clerklands and then steeply up again before easing off a little. From the stand of trees that marks the top of the hill, it's a pleasant roll for a mile down to the A7. There's really little choice but to stay with the A7 for the two miles into **Selkirk**.

The main square is the hub of the town and there is no shortage of shops and pubs. The Tourist Information Office is down an alley, just off the main square, and incorporates an interesting museum.

Leave the square on the road signed for Peebles and heading downhill. Immediately before the bridge over the Ettrick Water, turn right and, after a few yards, take the cycle track through the park on your left. Selkirk used to rely on the textile industry as its mainstay. It was not to last, though, and as you follow the river you can see the sites where proud mills once stood. New industries are developing, but the economy has never really recovered from the blow.

The track leads to a retail park and you need to join the cycle route alongside the A7 as far as the junction for Lindean. Turn left at the junction and follow what was the 'old' road as it crosses first the Ettrick and, further on, the Tweed near the point where the two rivers meet. Turn right now and follow the cycle route as it passes under the A7 and then alongside it towards Boleside.

This is now part of NCR1 and the route continues easily along the banks of the Tweed and past a picnic area. As you crest a slight rise the impressive Abbotsford House, home of Walter Scott, can be seen through the trees and across the river. And quite a home it must have been, too.

Pass under the road bridge and go straight on at a small roundabout. Look for signs on the right as you go uphill indicating the cycle track – you're still following the Tweed Cycleway. The track is known locally as the Black Path and follows the route of the former Waverley rail line. This section runs between Galashiels and Melrose; but with one small diversion. As you ride along here, the ever-present Eildons are up ahead offering you another of their many profiles to contemplate.

Pass an industrial estate on the left, and where the path meets a road ignore signs indicating the continuation of the cycle track and turn right instead to meet a T-junction. Turn left and cross the road to ride on what is another cycle path which leads to a roundabout. Follow the cycle path as it goes the 'wrong' way round the roundabout and heads towards the Borders General Hospital.

Where traffic turns off the main road and into the hospital there's an underpass, so use it and immediately turn right to pick up the trail on the opposite side of the road, running parallel to it. The track soon rejoins the course of the old railway and, in fact, you're about to arrive at Melrose Station, where the buildings and platform have been preserved. To reach the main square in **Melrose**, just go through the gate at the west end of the platform and head downhill.

17. Smailholm Tower

Distance:	34 miles
OS Maps:	Landranger 74
Start:	Kelso
Grade:	2
Surface:	road 30 miles/34 miles
	track 4 miles

The town of Kelso serves an agricultural area and was built around the abbey, founded in the early 12th century. It lies near the junction of the Tweed and the Teviot and, until relatively recently when the bypass was built, the impressive five-arched Rennie's bridge was the only way across the Tweed for several miles, both upstream and downstream. There's a wide variety of shops and facilities. Unusually, the market square and surrounding streets are cobbled and, if you don't have it already, you might be moved to consider the benefits of fitting suspension to your bike...

Leave the main square in **Kelso** by its northeastern corner. Shortly, you'll pass the ornate ceremonial gates of Floors Castle, the ancestral home of the Duke of Roxburgh. The estate borders the banks of the Tweed, but its landward boundaries are marked by a high stone wall, and it's this wall that you follow for a couple of miles. To get a glimpse of the castle and its grounds, which are open to the public, you can use the entrance which you'll pass soon after you turn onto the B6397. The estate and the impressive architecture of the castle have been the location for a number of films and it's easy to see why.

   This part of the route is following the Tweed Cycleway and, just where the road bears to the right, away from the estate wall, take a left turn for Makerstoun and follow the quiet lanes as they wend a route that eventually meets the B6404 road to St Boswells. The gaunt outline of Smailholm Tower dominates the scene and, to reach it, turn right and then left a little further along. An access road is signposted and passes through Sandyknowe farm.

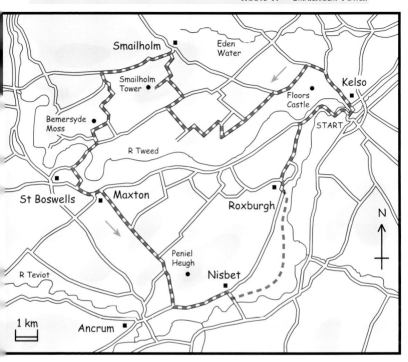

If you want to cut the trip short, then turn left on the B6404 and pick up the route again at Mertoun Bridge. This would take about seven miles off the total.

Smailholm Tower is built on a rocky outcrop and dates from the 15th century. There are fine views south to the Cheviots and west to the Eildons. The tower has been in the possession of several prominent local families. Sir Walter Scott's grandfather lived at the nearby farm, and Scott, a frequent visitor, writes of the tower in his book *Marmion*. It is now in the care of Historic Scotland.

Retrace your steps through the farm and head down towards **Smailholm** village. Follow minor roads for three miles or so to **Bemersyde Moss**, a wildlife reserve and home to many species of birds. For more information, and a unique insight to the area, look out for a

Roxburgh Viaduct, by Roxburgh village

wooden walkway on the right, just before the road takes a sharp left turn away from the Moss. The walkway leads to a birdwatchers' hide, built on stilts in the water, from which you can observe what's happening without being intrusive. It's a tranquil haven and a serene spot to sit and simply reflect a little.

Mertoun Bridge is the first crossing of the Tweed upstream from Kelso, and is where you head to next. Across the bridge you'll notice some steps on the left leading down to a path which follows the riverbank. It is possible to take the route along here to Maxton, but it's fairly tortuous and involves clambering up and down sets of steps. It's probably a better bet – and certainly an easier one – to carry on a little further and take the road on the left signposted for Benrig Cemetery and go round to **Maxton** that way.

Turn right at the end of the main street in the village and follow a gently undulating landscape towards the obvious Waterloo Monument that you can see ahead of you on Peniel Heugh. Access to the monument is by a fairly steep track which starts in some trees at (648 254), just before the road rolls downhill to meet the B6400.

Harestanes Woodland Visitor Centre is nearby, and you might wish to take a look at the local crafts on offer or drop into the tea rooms. In a similar vein, Monteviot House has gardens which are open to the public.

The route heads along to the small hamlet of **Nisbet**, where you have a choice: you can either stay with the road or follow the course of a disused rail track to Roxburgh. The rail track has a fairly good surface and would be my preferred option, since – like many of these routes – it gives a quite different perspective on the landscape that it passes through. When you get to what was Kirkbank Station the old bridge has gone, so you have to go down to the road then take some steps up to rejoin the track. Approaching **Roxburgh** village there's a fine view of the elegant viaduct which spans the Teviot over to your right.

The route continues towards the site of the old Roxburgh Castle, set on a hill in the triangular wedge of land where the Tweed and the Teviot converge. Turn right onto the main road and stop at a layby when Floors Castle comes into view – this is arguably the best place to view it from. To your right is the mound upon which Roxburgh Castle stood, and some historians are now claiming that even before the castle was built this was, in fact, the location of King Arthur's mythical kingdom of Camelot. Whatever the truth, this is an impressive site, being set between the two rivers, and it seems certain that the place has a wealth of stories to tell, were it only able to.

There is another story to be told, however, and if you look carefully you'll find a stone set into the grass just by the road at the foot of the mound. The inscription says that it's to the memory of three Polish soldiers who lost their lives 'while serving their country on Scottish soil' during the Second World War.

From here the road leads easily round to give picture-postcard views of **Kelso** and Rennie's bridge.

18. College Valley

Distance:	**26 miles**
OS Maps:	**Landranger 74, 80**
Start:	**Kirk Yetholm**
Grade:	**3**
Surface:	**road 18.5 miles**
	track 5.5 miles
	path 2 miles

College Valley cuts a prominent cleft through the northern part of the Cheviots and is the focus of this route. The highest point is at almost 500m, but despite this the going is surprisingly easy, with only a short section where you'll need to push. This is a magnificent area, but quite remote, so sensible precautions are advised.

Town Yetholm and Kirk Yetholm are close neighbours. Kirk Yetholm is at one end of the Pennine Way, and the Border Hotel is where those completing the route can claim their free drink for doing so. Town Yetholm is a little larger and has a couple of shops and pubs.

Curiously, Kirk Yetholm was home to a thriving Gypsy population, and it is said that one of the first schools for Romany children was set up here in 1850. This connection is evident today in the town's annual festival where the male and female 'figureheads' are respectively named the 'bari gadgi' and 'bari menushi'.

Leave **Kirk Yetholm**, passing the Border Hotel, on the road which skirts the northern edge of the Cheviot range. It's a bit of a plod round to Westnewton, where you turn in to College Valley. The surfaced road ends shortly after a small car park at Hethpool and reverts to track. You'll pass a monument dedicated to those who died in the 13 plane crashes that occurred in this area during the Second World War. Some wreckage can still be found on surrounding hills.

Bizzle Crags are ahead and to the left of you; **College Burn** stretches further up the valley, and that's where you're heading. At (877 212) the track forks, the route to the right being signed as a bridleway. It's actually easier to bear left here, passing a wood/corrugated iron shed. This

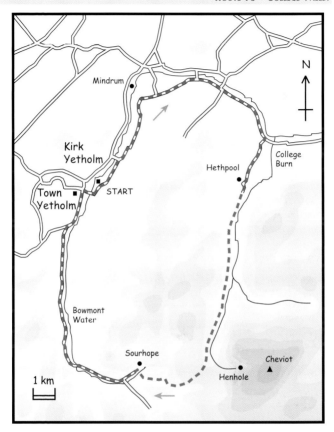

grassy track takes a diagonal route up the hillside to reach a col which stands on the Scottish/English border.

The obvious crags over to the left are situated in a hollow bowl known as the **Henhole** – a pleasant spot on a sunny day. You can't see the summit of the Cheviot from here, but the route joins the Pennine Way as it leads rightwards and up slightly towards the Refuge Hut which, incidentally, has been relocated from the position marked on some older maps.

Leaving the hut, go downhill for a short way until the main path bears right a little as it heads towards The Schil. Aim for a point where three fences meet. You need to keep the fence that runs southwest on your left as you set off down Auchope Rigg. There are a couple of steeper sections and, as always, please be aware of environmental issues and avoid churning the path. When you see the farm track, look for a flatter, grassy area and path leading down to meet it.

The track takes you to **Sourhope**, where it joins the minor road that follows **Bowmont Water** as it meanders gently down the valley and back into **Kirk Yetholm**.

19. Beadnell

Distance:	26 miles
OS Map:	Landranger 75
Start:	Embleton
Grade:	2 (or 1 if all road)
Surface:	road 23 miles/26 miles
	beach 3 miles

Another piece in the jigsaw that is the largely unspoilt Northumbrian coastline. The route includes about three miles cycling along beaches, and while you could stay with roads and avoid this, to do so would mean missing out on some of the best parts of the trip.

The village of **Embleton**, though quite small, has no less than three pubs. There's a campsite a little over half a mile to the south, and the area – in particular, the coast – is endowed with a wealth of hidden treasures and well worth exploring. There is a parking area by the Sportsman's Hotel on the road leading down towards the golf club and beach.

Turn your back on the sea – the beach section is left until last – and roll down through the village heading inland. Pass the Dunstanburgh Castle Hotel on your right and go straight ahead at the crossroads. This is now part of Route 1 of the National Cycle Network and follows quiet lanes on a circuitous stretch to Seahouses.

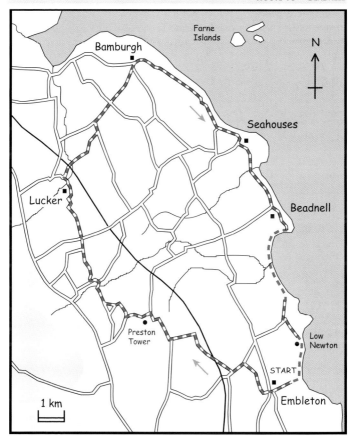

Look out for signs to **Preston Tower**. This is an old fortified 'Pele' house and was built over 600 years ago to protect the occupants in those troubled times. It is open to the public and the nominal charge helps with the upkeep. Fascinating snippets of history are recorded around the walls of the interior in an easily understood format. You learn, for example, that the practice of lighting fires against the outside wall, then piling on damp straw 'to smoke out the inmates', was known as 'scumfishing'.

Preston Tower, near Embleton

You might also be interested to follow the workings of the more recently installed clock mechanism, driven by the obvious large weights, and to see the Heath-Robinson linkages that are used to strike the huge bell on top of the tower. Go and take a look – the views of the surrounding countryside from the top are really quite fine. It's also worth noting that the grounds around the tower are home to an unusual collection of shrubs and trees.

Turn left as you leave Preston Tower and then right just after passing a school. This will bring you into the village of Ellingham. The Pack Horse Inn does bar snacks.

Follow the lanes as they trend northwards. Shortly after passing Low Nest, a right turn takes you onto a little-used road – it has grass growing up the middle of it and there are a couple of gates to pass through. Press on, though, and work your way to **Lucker**, which also has a pub, the Apple Inn.

It's about four miles now to **Bamburgh**, and the grandeur of the famous castle first comes into view just as you crest a slight ridge near Glororum. In the summer months, and particularly at weekends, the village can be quite busy with tourists. You might want to take a trip up to the lighthouse at Harkess Rocks and gaze out at the Farne Islands. It was Longstone, one of the islands furthest out, that was the scene of Grace Darling's celebrated rescue of survivors in 1838 when a ship struck the nearby Harcar Rock. Grace and her father, the lighthouse keeper on Longstone, launched their small rowing boat and took two trips in appalling weather to fetch people off the rock and to shelter. She died at an early age and was buried in the churchyard in Bamburgh. The Grace Darling Museum in the village houses an exhibition devoted to her life.

There is an inland route to **Seahouses**, but despite the extra traffic I think I prefer the coastal route for the views out to sea. Seahouses itself has a different character to Bamburgh and is more geared for tourism. The harbour is worth taking a peek at, and it's from here that boat trips to the Farne Islands can be arranged.

Moving down the coast, **Beadnell** is the next village. Where the main road turns inland, stay with the road that hugs the coast because you actually want to go round to the small harbour by the beach. Notice the old lime kilns just by the pier. Looking right down the coast from here, and well past the expanse of sand dunes, you can make out the outline of Dunstanburgh Castle in the distance. This obvious landmark will loom ever large as you move towards it.

If the tide is fully in then you could well be struggling to find a good line to cycle along the beach, and you might want to check this before you set out. At other times, though, the surface below the high-water mark is fairly compact. Half way along the beach a small river emerges from the dunes. At low tide you can cycle across it, but as the tide comes in you may need to wade across.

The beach from here on doesn't seem to be quite as firm, but it can be cycled all the way if you choose the right line. Don't go right to the end of the beach, but look for an access point 200 or 300 yards short of it leading through the dunes. It's just a short way to a small parking area.

This beach section can be avoided by using the path that runs behind the dunes – access to it is through the campsite. It should be noted, though, that this is designated as a footpath, and you don't therefore have the right to cycle along it.

Take the road now passing some low crags on the left. Turn left to take the road down to **Low Newton** by the Sea. This is a real delight, and consists of some cottages and a pub clustered round three sides of a grassy square by the beach. The Ship Inn does bar snacks and is probably as close as you'll get to a pub on the beach in this country. Difficult to beat on a sunny day.

The beach goes round a headland and there's a curious collection of holiday shacks up above the dunes. As you go further the almost Gothic outline of Dunstanburgh Castle appears even more stark. One of the towers looks as if it's about to fall over, but can't really be bothered; a strange sight indeed.

It's also possible to avoid this beach by using a path running behind the dunes. Access to the path is by turning right just before you get to the square at Low Newton and going round behind the cottages and pub. As before, though, it should be noted that this is a footpath, not a bridleway.

Again, a stream emerges from the dunes, and it's here that you'll need to walk your bike through the soft sand for a while until you reach the golf club, from where it's just a short way uphill to **Embleton**.

To avoid the section from Beadnell altogether, simply stay with the B1340 and follow the signs for Embleton.

20. Duchess's Drive

Distance:	21 miles
OS Map:	Landranger 73
Start:	Selkirk
Grade:	3
Surface:	road 11 miles
	track 8 miles
	path 2 miles

Waters from the Yarrow and Ettrick valleys merge just to the west of Selkirk, which sits proudly on a hill overlooking Ettrick Water. The textile industry was a mainstay of the area, but its decline, and that of a large and thriving electronics company in the town, dealt a blow to employment opportunities. The Tourist Information Centre, just off the main square down a narrow close, incorporates an interesting and well-designed museum, which is certainly worth a look if you have time.

Buccleuch Estates owns much of the land around here, and the liberal access policies of the current Duke are a welcome contrast to those of some other landowners. This route takes in part of the Duke's Bowhill Estate and, in particular, a section called Duchess's Drive.

From **Selkirk**'s main square take the road signed for Peebles and leading downhill. Look out for a sharp left turn for Ettrickbridge, which is easy to miss since it's just as you swoop round a left-hand bend. There's an uphill stretch before you get clear of the town and into open country.

About a mile past Oakwood Mill take the right turn signed for Bowhill, and immediately over the bridge turn left onto a track past some cottages. As you pass through trees you'll catch glimpses of Aikwood Tower on the other side of the river. This has been restored and houses an exhibition on the life and work of James Hogg – you'd need to check for opening times.

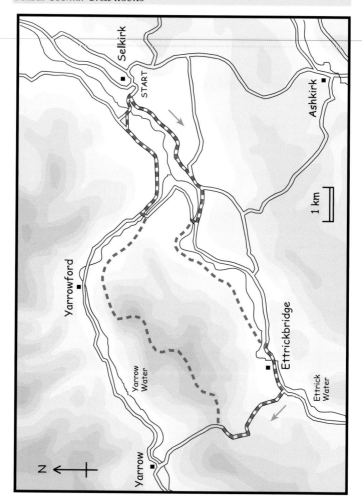

The track meets a surfaced road at Fauldshope, but soon reverts to its original state as you contour the hill towards Brockhill and Ettrickbridge. Pass by the cottages at Brockhill and cross the suspension bridge to reach the main road, from where it's just a few yards to the village. The Cross Keys on the main street in **Ettrickbridge** offers a good selection of food and drink.

Half a mile out of the village is the start of the road, known locally as the 'Bottom Swire', which climbs up and over to the Yarrow Valley. There's nothing for it but to get your head down and attack it as it weaves a line up the open hillside. The objective is clear, and so it's easy to gauge your progress. Kirkhope Tower is prominent over to the right, thought to have been the marital home of Mary Scott, immortalised in Border ballads as the 'Flower of Yarrow'.

Pause to catch your breath at the top of the hill and take in the views of the surrounding heather-clad hills.

You take the grassy hill track now. It starts by following the fence but diverges leftwards after a while. There's some up and down as the path works its way for a couple of miles to a point marked with a spot height of 474m. You'll see a track coming up the hill from Bowhill to the east. Aim to meet it, though it's possible to cut the corner as you do so, heading towards the summit of Fastheugh Hill. Don't actually go to the summit, though, but pass to the west of it to take a right fork at a junction.

This is Duchess's Drive, and there are good views along the ridge before dropping down and into the trees. The track joins a surfaced road near Newark Tower and it's worth taking just a slight detour at a left turn to go past it. The tower is mentioned by the Earl of Douglas in 1423 and, unlike some others, seems to have remained more or less intact since then.

It's about a mile along the road to the main entrance to Bowhill Estate, and the easiest route back from here is simply to follow the main road back into **Selkirk**.

21. Fatlips Castle

Distance:	40 miles
OS Maps:	Landranger 74, 80
Start:	Ancrum
Grade:	3
Surface:	road 40 miles

The village of Ancrum is the start point for a pleasant route, all on road, that circumnavigates the town of Jedburgh. It stays on quiet country lanes and shares some of them with the Four Abbeys cycle route. This is a fairly long trip, and Denholm is the only other village of any note that the route passes through, so make sure that you carry with you all that you need.

Ancrum has a triangular village green with a 16th-century market cross. The Cross Keys is the only pub, but it does have a good selection of beers. Head downhill from the green to cross the main A68 and take the road signed for Nisbet. A short way along here is the Harestanes Visitor Centre with its tea rooms and craft shows. Monteviot House Gardens are another local attraction and are open to the public.

You can't fail to notice the prominent Wellington Monument on top of Peniel Heugh, the hill to your left. It was built in 1815 as a tribute to the Duke of Wellington and is visible for many miles. The route here is actually part of the Four Abbeys cycle route, which weaves its way between the four abbeys of Kelso, Melrose, Jedburgh and Dryburgh.

Two miles past Nisbet, on the road to Roxburgh, is a right turn that leads down to follow the banks of the placid Teviot along to the elegant suspension bridge at Kalemouth. Turn right on the main road towards Jedburgh, but only for a few yards, before taking the road signed for Morebattle. Gentle gradients and low rolling hills typify the orderly rural landscape around here.

There is an off-road alternative from Nisbet that uses the old rail line towards Roxburgh village. This is shared with the Smailholm Tower route, and further details can be found there.

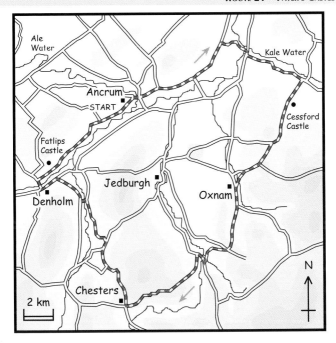

As you approach **Cessford**, a massively fortified castle can be seen on a prominent hill up to the left. It was probably built by the Ker family – one of the notorious Border reiving families of the time – in the middle of the 15th century, though like many other castles it was bombarded, partly demolished and rebuilt over the years. There's an interpretive plaque if you take the road up towards it, but the castle itself stands on private property and is not generally open to the public.

Turn left a couple of miles past Cessford to climb for a mile or so to a point where Dere Street, the old Roman road from York, crosses the hill on its way north towards Melrose and the fort at Trimontium by the Eildons. There are good views to the south and east from here.

Roll down to **Oxnam** ignoring a road off to the right. There's a gentle climb now before dropping down more steeply to Camptown on the main A68. Follow the main road north, but only for a few hundred yards to a left turn for Chesters. You'll pass the Jedforest Deer and Farm

Park as the road once again climbs gently upwards. Carter Bar is where the A68 crosses into England, and traffic can be seen snaking a path up the hillside to reach the border as you look to the south. Further to the west, and just a few miles south of Hawick, Leap Hill, though not particularly high, has a distinctive outline.

There's a pleasant cruise down to **Chesters**, where you turn right by the war memorial. More climbing – this time over Doorpool Hill – and as you drop down again Ruberslaw, another prominent hill, can be seen to the northwest. When you can see Ruberslaw to the left and the Eildons to the right, then Minto Crag appears about midway between them. Fatlips Castle is perched at the right-hand end of the crag.

As you follow the quiet lanes round to Bedrule, Ruberslaw dominates the skyline to the left. At one time there was a fort on the summit, but there's little evidence of that now. The low crags at the top of the hill provide a number of short routes for climbers.

Bedrule has its own war memorial on the right just as you approach the village. Turn left here, go down to cross Rule Water and then swing right to head for Denholm. You'll need to use the main road for the last half mile.

Denholm has a few shops, a couple of pubs and a large village green. From the green, a road leads down to the bridge over the Teviot. In the 18th century, and before the bridge was built, it seems that people would cross the river here using stilts, and most families would own at least one pair. Give the stilts a miss today, though, and take the bridge to turn right for Ancrum.

Passing along the foot of Minto Crag, you can't actually see **Fatlips Castle** until you're almost past it. The tower was built in the 16th century, and until relatively recently used to be in reasonable condition – one of the upper rooms, for example, had an ornately painted ceiling. Neglect and vandalism have taken their toll, though, and the building is now in a state of dereliction. It is, however, in a marvellous situation on top of the crag, and if you've time to take a stroll up the track which starts at (585 207) and leads up through the trees then your efforts will be well rewarded.

From Fatlips it's a leisurely four miles along the banks of the Teviot back to **Ancrum**.

22. Alemoor

Distance:	32 miles
OS Maps:	Landranger 73, 79
Start:	Ashkirk
Grade:	2
Surface:	road 32 miles

Ashkirk is a small village on the A7 about half way between Selkirk and Hawick. There's a pub but not much else, and nor should you rely on that being open. This route starts from the village, is all on road and takes in a mixture of valleys and open upland, some of which can be quite bleak in bad weather but, by the same token, exhilarating on a sunny day.

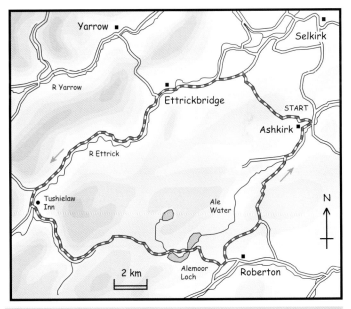

Take the road out of **Ashkirk** heading uphill for the Ettrick Valley. This is called the Woll. It's a fairly stiff haul for a while before emerging onto the Woll Rigg with open views in all directions. The familiar outline of the Eildons catches the eye to the northeast. This is upland pasture and, as the road starts to go downhill, the large estate and mansion that you can see ahead of you across the valley is Bowhill. It belongs to the the Duke of Buccleuch, as does much of the land hereabouts.

Turn left at the T-junction and you'll reach the main road up the Ettrick Valley after a mile. Traffic is usually light and gets less the further up the valley you go. Aikwood Tower is on the left as you near Ettrickbridge. It has been restored by David Steel – formerly MP for the area – and now houses an exhibition to James Hogg, the Ettrick Shepherd. Opening times vary, so you would be advised to check in advance if you plan to call in.

Ettrickbridge is a pleasant village, and the local pub, the Cross Keys, can be recommended.

It's a fair way along the Ettick now to the **Tushielaw Inn**, an old pub, but one which rarely seems open when I pass it. Turn left here to follow the Rankle Burn up a winding valley before heading gently uphill. Craik Forest is over to the right, and almost at the top of the hill, opposite an entrance to the forest, you'll find a small cairn marking the spot of what once was Redfordgreen School. It opened in 1885 and closed in 1955, and it would be difficult to imagine a bleaker place in winter on which to site a place of learning.

Go past **Alemoor Loch** and, as you head just slightly upwards, the Eildons are again prominent to the northeast. Dropping into Borthwickdale you can make out Ruberslaw to the east and, beyond that, the Cheviot Hills.

Don't go as far as Roberton but, instead, take the left turn for Ashkirk and climb to a junction at Blawearie. You're on open moorland now, and hills and heather dominate the scene for miles around. It is easy cruising along here, but keep an eye out for a cairn on the right built as a memorial to local poet Will Ogilvie. Will died in 1963, but the cairn is a relatively recent addition. One of his poems is called 'The Road to Roberton' and, looking around, you can perhaps see why he chose to write about it.

Take care as you head quite steeply downhill as there's a bend at the bottom. Cross the **Ale Water** and coast along the valley back to **Ashkirk**.

River Tweed and Kelso town (Route 17)

Auchope Refuge, Cheviot Hills (Route 18)

Bridge at Towford, Cheviot Hills (Route 23)

23. Border Ridge

Distance:	18 miles
OS Map:	Landranger 80
Start:	Hownam
Grade:	5
Surface:	road 4 miles
	track 2 miles
	path 12 miles

A demanding, but tremendously rewarding, route in remote country taking you high into the Cheviot Hills, along the Border Ridge and returning via The Street, an old Roman road. The area is isolated and quite featureless in places, so you are advised that navigation is an issue to consider. The Ordnance Survey 'Outdoor Leisure' series includes a 1:25000 double-sided map of the Cheviot Hills which can be recommended for this and other routes in the area.

Hownam isn't the easiest place to get to, nor will you find much when you arrive. If you're travelling by car – and there's little alternative – then you could leave it in a small grassy lay-by at (780 188). Retrace your route towards the village just a little and turn left at the junction to head south towards Towford.

This road isn't a dead-end, but you're unlikely to be troubled by much in the way of traffic. In fact, the valley has a grandeur of its own. Much of it is unfenced pasture, and **Kale Water** carves a leisurely line through the middle of it all. It's one of these places that takes on a mood, depending on the season and the weather, ranging from welcoming summer sunshine to surly winter gloom.

Four miles brings you to **Towford**, and this is the only road you're going to use on this trip or, at least, the only surfaced one. The Roman road running from York to Edinburgh is called Dere Street, and it passes through here, probably crossing the river just where the ford is now, before heading north over the hill towards Whitton Edge. You're going to follow it in the opposite direction up onto the ridge to the southeast,

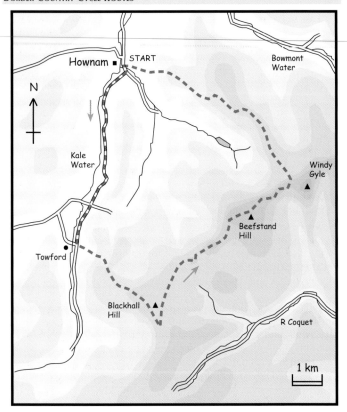

and if you look up the line of the route you'll see a stone hut on the skyline.

The path goes through a couple of gates. I suppose there are those who would see it as a challenge to cycle this section, but I'm not one of them, and resign myself to the walk. Don't, by the way, be fooled into thinking that the hut marks the Border Ridge. It doesn't, and there's more to do yet. Equally, though, don't let that put you off, because this is the hardest part and the difficulties will ease when you reach the hut.

Pass to the right of the stone hut and take a moment or two to get your bearings as the scene unfolds. The trail now works its way round to the right a little, towards the head of the valley that drops away to your left. You'll come to a fork near a gate. The left-hand fork rises towards the prominent Greyhen Rock, while your route goes straight ahead through the gate – it may even be signed for Dere Street.

The path now is quite narrow and contours round the hillside as another valley drops away quite steeply to the right. If you look over to the west, you can probably pick out traffic in the distance as it crawls its way across the border at Carter Bar. You're aiming to join the Pennine Way, which runs along the Border Ridge. It has wooden marker posts every so often and it should be fairly obvious when you come across the junction. Cut back on yourself now to follow the Way as it moves north, then veers to the east, over featureless heather-clad hillside.

On the way you'll find sections of the route which have been 'paved' with natural flagstones in an effort to avoid erosion and damage. The 'fun' aspect of this is that it may sharpen your skills as you negotiate them, but I would ask, of course, that you give some consideration to the environmental issues, as these seem to become more contentious each year.

At the top of a small hill – I'd hesitate to call it a summit – the fence and the route take a sharp left turn, and you can see the Yearning Saddles Mountain Refuge just down the hill a little. As with all refuges, if you have something useful that you could contribute to it then that is appreciated. Take a look inside; perhaps you'd like to sign the guest book.

You can be in little doubt that the next section up Lamb Hill is not one that you'll be cycling, so there's nothing for it but to get the head down and work your way up to the top. The gradient is easier now and, even though **Beefstand Hill** requires a tad more work, there can surely be even less doubt that the effort is well worth it, and that the scene that you see all around you from this high point of 560m is one to savour.

Mozie Law is the last hill before dropping down to a 'crossroads' at (836 155) where The Street crosses the border. It is signposted. So the Pennine Way continues along towards **Windy Gyle** and eventually its destination of Kirk Yetholm. Those who have walked over 200 miles to get this far must be starting to see light at the end of the tunnel.

Head off to the northwest, then, but don't expect this last section to **Hownam** to be quite the breeze you might like it to be. The surface isn't always solid, and the route takes a few twists and turns along the way, not to mention a few ups and downs. The track does improve as you get nearer the village, and it is to be hoped that you still have some wear left on the brake pads because there are some steeper sections. Enjoy it, though, because this has been a hard day's work – but worth every bit of it.

24. Grey Mare's Tail

Distance:	**40 miles**
OS Maps:	**Landranger 73, 78, 79**
Start:	**Gordon Arms Hotel**
Grade:	**5**
Surface:	road 34 miles
	track 3 miles
	path 3 miles

A superb route passing through some of the finest that the Southern Uplands has to offer. It starts in the Yarrow Valley, crosses over into the Ettrick and up to its watershed on the Southern Upland Way. You then drop down in spectacular fashion to Moffat Water and follow the route up and past the waterfalls of the Grey Mare's Tail to cross over back into the Yarrow Valley and St Mary's Loch. Because of the remoteness of the upland part of the route, some consideration should be given to appropriate mountain clothing and equipment.

There are a number of starting points, depending on where you're travelling from: the Grey Mare's Tail itself, possibly, if you're coming from the Moffat direction. Tibbie Shiels Inn by St Mary's Loch is another. I started at the **Gordon Arms Hotel**, and the route is described from there. If you leave a car there, then it's always a good idea to call in at the end of the day and offer some custom in return – you'll likely be in need of some refreshment anyway!

There's a steady pull of about four miles as you cross from Yarrow to Ettrick. The gradient is easy enough, but a southwesterly of any strength would make it a mite tedious. At the watershed the road turns sharp left. The track off to the right leads down to join the Captain's Road and then

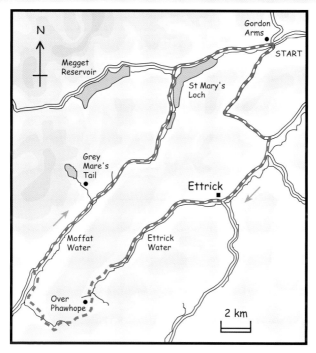

emerges by Tibbie Shiels Inn on St Mary's Loch. Your route, though, rolls down into the Ettrick Valley at Tushielaw.

After half a mile you'll pass Tushielaw Inn, though I wouldn't rely on it being open. This would have been an important droving route – it's at a strategic junction hereabouts – but nowadays there's only minimal traffic.

Follow Ettrick Water and turn off to the village of **Ettrick**. Just by the school is a monument to the birthplace of James Hogg, the Ettrick Shepherd. Hogg, Sir Walter Scott and other members of the Edinburgh literati of the time would sometimes gather at Tibbie Shiels Inn for what has been described elsewhere as a 'weekend of bucolic bonding'. Tibbie – or Isabella, as she was properly known – who ran the inn, had, it seems, a rare skill in keeping them all under control.

Both Tibbie and Hogg were buried in the kirkyard at Ettrick. Hogg's grave has a large headstone and is directly south of the church tower next to that of his grandfather, Will O' Phaup, who 'for feats of frolic, agility and strength had no equal in his day', according to the inscription on the stone. More details of Will's colourful exploits – some of them amusing and some sad – can be found in Hogg's *Tales of the Ettrick Shepherd*.

It's a good few miles up the valley, but at no point strenuous, to the end of the tarred road just near Potburn. You've actually been following the Southern Upland Way for a while now and it continues on the track ahead. Shortly after Potburn, and just at a stream crossing, is **Over Phawhope** Bothy. This bothy has always been well respected and kept in good condition, and it is to be hoped that it will continue to avoid the vandalism that has so plagued other bothies in recent (and not-so-recent) years. If you can help in any way – by checking it, or contributing something of use – then that is appreciated.

The track now climbs gently through the trees to approach Ettrick Head – be sure to spot the signed path on the left that takes you through trees and out onto grassy slopes. Continue to a stile which marks the boundary between Dumfries & Galloway and Scottish Borders.

There's a real feeling of isolation. Hills are all around but, equally, I've been here when the cloud has been right down making a compass an essential piece of kit.

The path heads downwards, gently at first but then more steeply into a grassy gully. Cross the Selcoth Burn at a small wooden bridge. You'll need to push when the path takes an uphill turn and the gully walls steepen. Back on grassy slopes again, make your way down to the col above where the Selcoth Burn swings sharp right and down through steep valley walls. The Southern Upland Way continues southwest, but you head northwest traversing high above the burn. Don't even think of cycling this, as there are serious drops off to the right and the path is only narrow.

Moving further down the valley, keep a lookout for a grassy track on the opposite (right) bank of the stream. When you see it, find a suitable crossing point and make your way over the burn and up to the track. Difficulties ease now, and you can roll easily down to join the farm access track. Turn right to pass a fish farm and then cross the **Moffat Water** to go up to the main road.

This is a classic U-shaped valley, and as you look back to where

St Mary's Loch

you came from you'll appreciate the improbable line that you've just followed down into it.

Although this is a main road, it carries relatively light traffic. Enjoy the scenery as you near the **Grey Mare's Tail**. You can see the waterfalls from the road, but the best, and only, approach is on foot – there's a low-level route to the left and a steep path to the right. In any event, take care as lives have been lost here.

The road, though narrow, leads fairly easily up to the head of the valley and, once again, across the regional boundary into Scottish Borders and the Yarrow Valley. There's an easy cruise now for two or three miles to the Loch of the Lowes. This loch flows into **St Mary's Loch**, and between the two is the legendary Tibbie Shiels Inn. If you take a detour and look in the bar there's a framed photograph on the wall which, it is said, clearly shows a ghostly image of Tibbie herself…

Back on the main road is yet another monument to James Hogg; this time a statue of the man himself accompanied by his faithful dog Hector as they gaze over the waters of St Mary's Loch.

The Southern Upland Way follows the eastern shore of the loch. If you want to give it a try – and there's a fair bit of walking involved – then access is through the sailing club behind Tibbie's. It's easier, and no less scenic, to stay with the road. A couple of miles or so past the far end of the loch brings you back to the **Gordon Arms** and the end of a fine day out.

25. Salters Road

Distance:	40 miles
OS Maps:	Landranger 80, 81
Start:	Ingram
Grade:	5
Surface:	road 24 miles
	track 15 miles
	path 1 mile

This is a fairly lengthy – and strenuous in places – route through the Northumberland National Park. It takes in exposed hills where the consequences of an accident or injury could be quite serious, so the undertaking deserves a little respect on that basis alone.

The idea is to work your way around to the Coquet Valley, follow it for a few miles, then take a route up and over the hills to drop down into the upper Breamish Valley and wend your way back down to the start. If you're lucky enough to be blessed with sunny weather then it really does make a superb day out. Enjoy!

One of the 'entrances' to the national park is the Breamish Valley road to **Ingram**. There's a visitors centre just by the village and you could start the route from there. Alternatively, there is a large grassy area a mile and a half or so before you reach Ingram, by a ford at Brandon. The route is described from here.

Cross the ford – or take the bridge if you prefer – and follow the track to Brandon. Join the road which rises to Mile End Farm. There are several possibilities to get you to Alwinton. The route drops down now into the Vale of Whittingham and crosses the River Aln. Turn right, keeping the rather stately Eslington Park to your right and heading for Ryle Mill and Little Ryle.

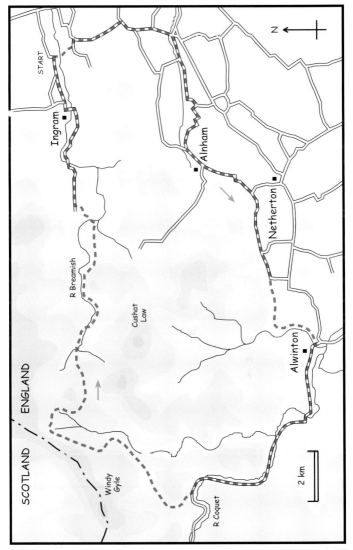

When you reach **Alnham** you're contouring around the foothills and following the boundary of the national park. Pass through Biddlestone, keeping to the road as it clings to the foot of the slopes. The road takes a sharp left turn, just before Rookland, but you carry straight on along the grassy track. It's fairly flat for a while, but soon starts to drop towards the campsite at Clennell Hall. The hall is named after Clennell Street, the old Roman road which passes near to here as it goes north from Alwinton to cross the border into Scotland.

Pass around the back of the main building and follow the track along to join the main road into **Alwinton**. The village itself is neat and picturesque with its sandstone cottages and tiny pub. It is the gateway to Upper Coquetdale, and this is a real treasure of a valley. It's effectively a dead-end, so traffic is only minimal as the road meanders along by the river.

The MOD firing ranges of Otterburn are up and over to your left, so you can sometimes hear the dull thump of explosions if the army is testing its latest weapons. For the most part, though, this is a tranquil corner of Northumberland, and the steeply sloping hillsides heighten the sense of anticipation as you make your way up the twists and turns of the valley.

Look for a track on the right signed for Uswayford – pronounced 'oozyford' – and follow it as it works its way up this side valley. The track is a good one and gains height steadily. To the north is **Windy Gyle** and the Border Ridge, along which runs the Pennine Way.

Uswayford is a farm steading near the head of this valley, but you need to look for a track on the left leading off into the trees about half a mile short of the farm buildings. In fact, you're aiming for a point up the hill directly behind Uswayford, as you look at it from here, but the track that you're going to follow rises gently and takes a long contour around the head of the valley to reach the high point of the route at about 470m. Despite being in forest it's quite open, and there are views which enable you to keep a bearing on where you're heading. Eventually, you will come across a wooden sign pointing to Salters Road West – which, it has to be said, doesn't look too inviting – and Salters Road East, which is the one you want.

There's nothing to be gained by following the forest track any further, since it stops at a turning circle after just a few yards. Take to the path as it works across through the heather towards a fence. This is truly a fine spot to be as your gaze moves from the hills around you to the views that are now opening up of the remote valley that you're about to descend. The first time I came here, I had no idea whether the route was going to 'go' or not, so there was a sense of relief to find that it would, and also a sense of awe at the surroundings. This, after all, is the middle of a national park and I hadn't seen another soul since leaving the road; nor did I until rejoining it further down the valley.

The grassy track isn't too obvious and is quite steep as you move off downhill. If in doubt, keep over to the left. The route takes you to a junction of two streams and a small wooden bridge crossing one of them. Join the track now as it leads down past High Bleakhope to Low Bleakhope – probably apt names in the depths of winter. Here the river, and the track, swing sharply to the left. Salters Road, in fact, continues up the hill straight ahead, but you turn left to stay with the river.

The track starts to climb up the hillside, quite steeply in places, before dropping down again to cross the river at Alnhammoor. It's a short climb now up to the surfaced road at Hartside. If you have time, and energy, you might want to go along to Linhope and take a walk up to the waterfalls there. In any event, you've now got a real treat of a roll back down the valley to **Ingram** and along to the ford at Brandon. Take time, though, to call in at the visitor centre on the way.

26. Amble

Distance:	26 miles
OS Map:	Landranger 81
Start:	Alnmouth
Grade:	2
Surface:	road 22 miles/23 miles
	track 2 miles/3 miles
	beach 2 miles

The Northumberland coastline is amongst the finest in the country. There are beaches that stretch for miles with scarcely a person to be seen. Sand dunes, coves and cliffs, all waiting to be discovered. This route takes in just a small section of the coast and the three towns of Alnmouth, Warkworth and Amble on the way before returning via an inland route. There is an option to cycle some way along the beach, though you can avoid this if you wish.

Alnmouth, like most of the coastal towns hereabouts, manages to avoid the more tacky trappings associated with many resorts elsewhere in the country. It is geared for tourism, in a modest sort of way, but welcomes visitors on its own terms.

Leave the town crossing the Duchess Bridge and aiming for the main road south. Look for the cycle route which runs parallel to the main road. You can follow this all the way to Warkworth and, indeed, this is the easier option.

If you're game for two miles along the beach then stay with the route following the main road until you see stony track leading down towards the dunes. You'll need to force a route through them to the beach but there is an alternative landward track.

The compactness of sand is a major factor when cycling a beach and they do seem to vary widely in this respect. Often a good line is to stick close to the high water mark; sometimes it's better if the tide is out a little so that you can cycle as far down the beach as possible and

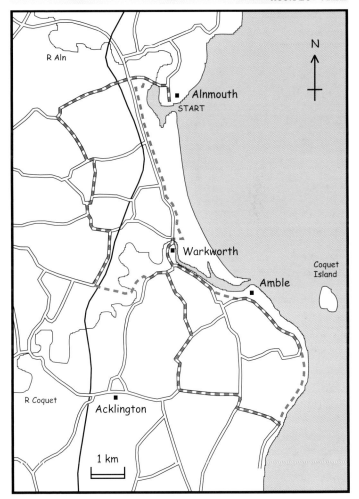

close to, if not actually in, the water. You've simply got to try it and see. But there's no doubt that it really can be tremendous fun given decent conditions.

Warkworth

There are some rocks at Birling Carrs, but these present no difficulty. The profile of Coquet Island stands out further down the coast.
Don't go to the end of the beach. You're looking for an access point
by a golf course which is marked by a lifebelt on a post. This leads
directly to Warkworth

If, instead, you stay with the track behind the dunes then it leads
you up to the main road just before reaching the golf course.

The track leads directly into **Warkworth**, and you can't fail to be
impressed by the old bridge which spans the River Coquet and takes
you to the main street, at the top of which is Warkworth Castle. Its pres-
ence dominates the town as it stands brooding over it.

If you want to wash the sand off your bike then it's possible to nip
down to the river just behind the church. The town bears some exploration if you're not in too much of a hurry, and the castle, of course, has
a rich – and sometimes bloody – history of its own.

The main road follows the River Coquet as it nears its journey's end. The harbour is always full of interest, and just as the road veers off to the right you can take a path along the river that leads past the marina and into **Amble** town centre. It has a different character to Warkworth, but there's plenty to see if you poke around.

Try to pick the coast road out of town. Notice a lonesome spire surrounded by a small graveyard. Apparently there used to be two chapels of rest, one either side of it…one was for Catholics, the other for Protestants. Some things never change.

The road turns to track and then singletrack for a short way as you go through part of Druridge Bay Country Park. The empty sands of Druridge Bay stretch away for as far as you can see to the south and, in fact, this is probably the longest beach in Northumberland. Soon the track turns back to road and there's a right turn inland at Hadston Carrs.

The route back is a little devious but provides some interest. Turn right at the main road and then almost immediately left towards Togston. Follow the lanes aiming for Warkworth, and as you approach the town you'll come to a T-junction by a cricket pitch. Turn left for 500 yards and then look for Watershaugh Road on the right, entering leafy suburbia.

This may look a little unlikely, but the route leads round to the left then drops down to a ford. This particular ford can be a tad intimidating, as it is often quite wide and the water can be fairly fast flowing. It shouldn't be too deep unless there's been a lot of rain, but there is a footbridge downstream a little if you have any doubts. The best approach, in my view, is to a) accept that you're going to get wet feet, and b) don't focus on the water in front of your wheels, but concentrate on where you're aiming for, and c) keep pedalling! Be assured that any sand still attached to your bike won't be there for long.

It's uphill now, past a caravan site. Turn right just over the railway and take minor roads heading north and trending gently upwards to a high point near an MOD installation on top of a hill. The RAF announce, rather cheekily, that it's guarded by geese. Turn right at the junction and relax as you coast downhill back to **Alnmouth**. As you cross the Duchess Bridge, you'll notice a path on the right going along the river called 'Lovers Walk', which may be worth exploring.

27. Otterburn Range

Distance:	33 miles
OS Maps:	Landranger 80, 81
Start:	Alwinton
Grade:	3
Surface:	road 19 miles
	track 14 miles

Upper Coquetdale is part of the Northumberland National Park, one of northern England's lesser-known treasures, and gives access to a number of fine routes. The valley doesn't carry through traffic, and is worth exploring in its own right as its twists and turns lead you towards the source of the River Coquet. This route also crosses the army's restricted firing range and clearly you would need to check beforehand to make sure that they're not firing. Details of how to do this are given elsewhere in the guide.

The village of **Alwinton** – no shop, one pub – is the start point, and there is a small parking area and public toilets. The valley is quite open here, but as you move further up it narrows a little and the hillsides become steeper and take on a more remote 'feel' to them. To the left is the firing range, though most of it is hidden from view. One or two routes take off up valleys to the right, but you're aiming to get almost to the head of the valley. The road crosses, and re-crosses, the river; gradients are reasonable for most of the way, but there are one or two fairly fierce hills to tackle. There is a height gain of around 250m as you go up the valley, and where the public road ends you're at a height of about 400m.

The course of Dere Street runs past here as it forces a route northwards, and the remains of a Roman camp can be seen on the hillside just up ahead. The Pennine Way, though not quite as old, also passes by and leads up onto the Border Ridge. Access to the ridge from the English side is relatively straightforward using this route, though you do need to push for parts of it. You could link, then, with the Borders Ridge route to give you plenty of scope for exploration.

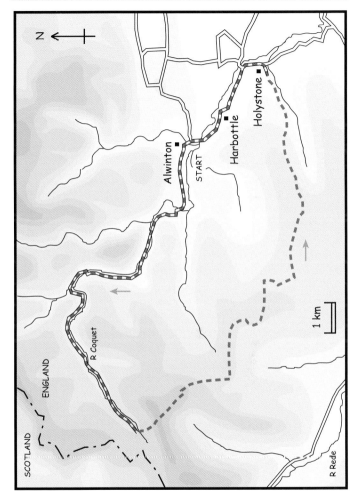

Your route turns left to head steeply up along the MOD road. I've classed this as a 'track', but in fact the road is surfaced and well-maintained. The short but brutal climb brings you to over 500m, and if you've energy enough to lift your eyes then they're in for a treat as you survey the landscape from this lofty and isolated spot. The area is used for testing artillery shells, and you can see evidence of this as you travel through it.

You can relax now as you head more easily to a T-junction, reached after a mile or so. Turn left here and roll downhill to another T-junction at (818 042). Turn left again and there's a gentle climb before easy cycling takes you round to yet another junction at (864 013), passing the old rusting hulk of some military hardware on the way.

It isn't quite downhill all the way to **Holystone**, but it is for most of it. From here you've got about three miles along the road to Alwinton, passing through **Harbottle** on the way.

28. Kielder

Distance:	42 miles
OS Map:	Landranger 80
Start:	Kielder Village
Grade:	4
Surface:	road 16 miles
	track 15.5 miles
	path 10.5 miles

This is quite a long trip through some remote and isolated country, so allow plenty of time and try to pick decent weather – there are some bleak stretches here. It's also fair to say that there are some pretty relentless climbs, but don't let that put you off because you won't regret taking the time, and making the effort, to explore the area. Two suggested starting points for the route are at Kielder and at a picnic spot a couple of miles southeast of Byrness on the A68. The route is described from Kielder.

There's a Visitor Centre at Kielder Castle and it's worth having a nose around if you've time. The castle used to be a hunting lodge belonging to the Duke of Northumberland. Kielder Water, of course, is man-made and the whole area is being promoted for tourism. Water sports are popular, as is cycling and there are a number of marked trails through

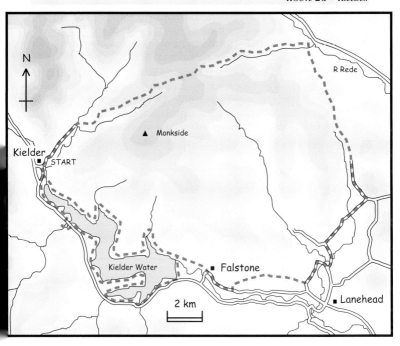

the forests. More are being developed and details are available at the information centre and also online.

The first part of the route runs along the length of Kielder Water so you can use the recently constructed Lakeside Way which runs right round the lake. You can choose either the north or south shore route; both are good cycle paths. The north shore is shorter but the south shore may be easier in terms of height gain and loss.

The route distances quoted are for the north shore route and you'll need to add on about 2.5 miles if following the south shore.

If you're starting from the car park at the visitor centre then go downhill and turn left at the bottom to cross a river and pass the youth hostel on the left. Work your way through the housing scheme kinking right then left. The trail for the north shore is on the left just before crossing the Kielder Burn. If you're taking the south shore route then continue on the road for a few hundred yards and your trail starts again on the left. Both routes are purpose built and offer good views of the lake. You'll also pass points of interest, art installations and so on, but best to discover these for yourself...

If you follow the north shore you'll end up in a car park at the northern end of the dam. If you take the southern route then cycling across the dam will bring you to the same place.

Take the obvious signed route out of the car park which goes downhill quite steeply and then joins the course of the old railway. This is my kind of gradient and leads easily to **Falstone**. Access to the village – shop and pub – is under the rail bridge, but your route takes the road that climbs along the hillside. The scene has changed altogether now, from the harsh conifer plantation and rough track along the lake to a more gentle river valley and grassy hillside.

Still rising, the road reaches a prominent clump of old pine trees. Here again, there's a choice. Both the Reivers Way and the Border County Ride follow the track that heads uphill to the left. The track starts off with a good surface, but this won't last for too long. In a good spell of weather there isn't a problem, but the trail can get a little muddy in places if there's been recent rain. Once past Slaty Ford and its waterfall the track will start to improve until eventually it rejoins the surfaced road at a junction.

You can avoid this part of the route by staying on the road. It passes through a number of gates and you'll lose some height. Turn left just up the hill past Rushend and rejoin the route at the junction.

The narrow road leads gently up to crest a rise just near a gate. Views unfold and again the character of the landscape seems to take on an open upland feel to it. Hills roll away in the distance, although the mood can be quite menacing in poor weather. Roll downhill to another gate by a lone cottage and the road rounds a corner to St Aidan's church, an evangelical outpost in these wide open spaces.

There is some hard work to come in following the lanes as they trend inexorably upwards, and quite steeply in places, to a T-junction near Pit Houses at (816 917). This is open moorland at about 300m, and the route now aims towards the forest, away to the north. Still climbing, the surfaced road ends as you reach the edge of the forest and reverts to track.

The Pennine Way joins the route as the track reaches a col at about 350m. From here you can enjoy some reward for your efforts as the trail leads down to the obvious picnic area by the River Rede.

There's another long, but not too strenuous, haul along the forest track to the high point of the trip at Blakehope Nick. You're at around 450m, and you'll want to pause a while and take in the scenery around this vast expanse. The hard work is over, and you can relax and enjoy the long run back down to **Kielder**.

29. Eskdalemuir

Distance:	**22 miles/24 miles**
OS Map:	**Landranger 79**
Start:	**Eskdalemuir**
Grade:	**1**
Surface:	**road 20.5 miles/24 miles**
	track 0.5 mile
	path 1 mile

The small village of Eskdalemuir is the start for this route, which takes in part of the upper Esk Valley. It runs through open upland and forested areas, and there are plenty of opportunities for exploring forestry trails in the area. The route is all on road, but there is a possible shortcut over tracks.

Start by the church in **Eskdalemuir** and head uphill going west on the B723. The top of this uphill section is where forestry land begins on both sides of the road, and there are a number of tracks leading off to the left and right. Coming out of the trees you can look forward to a pleasant cruise downhill to **Boreland**.

There is a climb now, and quite steep to begin with, before dropping down to cross Corrie Water and yet another climb to **Corrie Common**. There are good views from here to the west and southwest to the north Lakes hills. You drop down to **Paddockhole** and turn left to climb back up. There is a shortcut, though…

At the last house on the left at Corrie Common there's a track sign-posted for a picnic area near some kennels. Take the track heading downhill. It emerges from the trees shortly, goes over open land and then

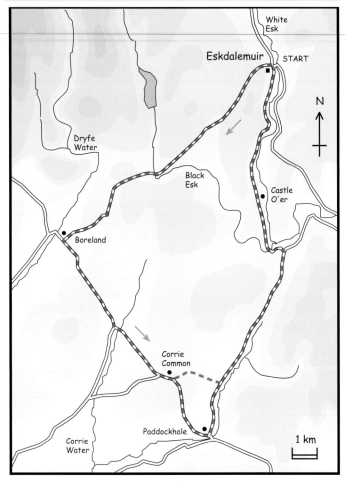

crosses a small stream just by the corner of a forested area. A vague path goes off to the right. It comes out by an old farm building, and you need to take a line aiming for some white farm buildings ahead of you on the hillside opposite. This will bring you down to join the road at a gate.

This is an open upland road and pretty well devoid of traffic. Turn left at Bailiehill for a fine run down to the junction of the White Esk and Black Esk. There's a parking and picnic area and, again, the woodland trails are well worth exploring. It's four or five miles on the **Castle O'er** road back to **Eskdalemuir**.

30. Newcastleton

Distance:	31 miles
OS Map:	Landranger 79
Start:	A7, north of Langholm
Grade:	3
Surface:	road 31 miles

A circular tour, all on tarmac, taking in the moorland road that connects Langholm to Newcastleton, going further up the Liddesdale Valley then crossing more hills to rejoin the A7 a few miles north of Langholm. There are some strenuous climbs, but these are compensated for by stunning views of the surrounding hills.

Unfortunately, there is a section of several miles along the main A7 which can't really be avoided unless you can arrange some sort of transport. Part of this section of A7 has a cycle track and other parts offer the 'protection' of a solid white line, but the rest of it doesn't, and this may be a factor in deciding how to tackle it.

Another factor to consider is the wind direction and which way round to do the route. The main haul is the road between Langholm and Newcastleton, and you might want to think about the merits of a following wind here. I decided to do the section along the A7 first, and the route is described from the junction of the A7 and the road to Hermitage. You can leave a car at (394 965).

It's almost eight miles to Langholm along the main road; just over a mile of this is on a dedicated cycle track. Unless you particularly want to go into the town, take the road to Newcastleton on the left just before reaching **Langholm**. This is steep to start with, but the gradient eases a little as you come out of the trees.

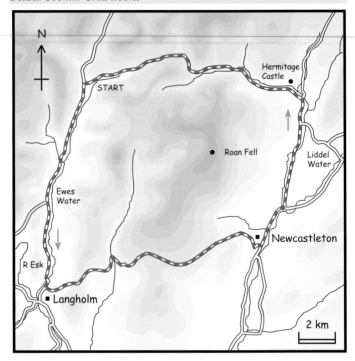

Towards the top of the hill you'll come across the rusting hulk of a sculpture erected to the memory of the poet Hugh MacDiarmid. There's a track off to the right leading towards the much more imposing monument that you can see on top of the hill. This is the Malcolm monument, so called in tribute to a local military hero of that name. The views from the hill here are worth the mile and a half round detour to get there. To the west and south you can see the Solway Firth and hills of the northern Lake District. To the north is a fine view along upper Eskdale.

The road continues and heads down slightly to Tarras Lodge before climbing again to a high point of about 340m. This is open country and the views are extensive – reward for your efforts in getting here. It's a real treat of a run now for a few miles down into **Newcastleton**.

If you've visited Tomintoul in the Grampians you'll be struck by the almost identical layout of the long main street and square in the town. In fact both were designed as 'planned villages', but by different people. Newcastleton was created by the Duke of Buccleuch in 1793, almost 20 years after Tomintoul, but you can't help thinking there's a connection somewhere. Anyway, there are shops and a couple of hotels if you want to take a look around the town.

Leave the square heading north towards Hawick. After about six miles there's a left turn for **Hermitage Castle**, whose imposing structure soon looms into view, and you may want to spend some time looking around it. Mary Queen of Scots is said to have ridden 50 miles in a day, from Jedburgh to here and back, to visit her wounded lover the Earl of Bothwell, and causing some scandal in the process.

You still have a watershed to cross at the head of this quiet valley, but it isn't as strenuous as the one over from Langholm. The high point is at the end of some forestry on the right, and it really is a delightful cruise from here down to the A7.

31. Bloody Bush Road

Distance:	**38 miles**
OS Maps:	**Landranger 79, 80**
Start:	**Kielder Visitor Centre**
Grade:	**4**
Surface:	**road 10 miles**
	track 25 miles
	path 3 miles

Kielder Forest is a catch-all name generally used to describe a vast area just south of the Scottish border. In fact, Kielder Forest itself is surrounded by Wauchope and Redesdale Forests to the north, Falstone Forest to the east, Spadeadam and Wark Forests to the south and Kershope and Newcastleton Forests to the west. The boundaries between them are not always distinct or obvious, but much of the area is open to walkers and cyclists. Efforts are being made to introduce a wider variety of forest plantings, which include areas of broad-leaved trees as well as the more ubiquitous blanket conifer.

Kielder Water is a man-made reservoir and was created in the early 1980s, submerging a large area of land which, sadly from my point of view, included a rather likeable crag called The Belling in the process. Fortunately, fairly liberal access policies have been pursued, and tourism – which takes advantage of facilities for water sports, walking and cycling – has been actively encouraged. The area's remoteness, though, ensures that crowds are never a problem, and there is no shortage of wild and empty countryside for all to make use of.

Your route here starts at the **Kielder** Visitor Centre at Kielder Castle. The castle was built in 1775 by the then Duke of Northumberland as a hunting lodge. The exhibitions in the centre are worth a visit in their own right. There's also a pub and some tea rooms. Cycle hire is an option if required. It's also worth noting that the village can be reached from the A68 via a (toll) forest road.

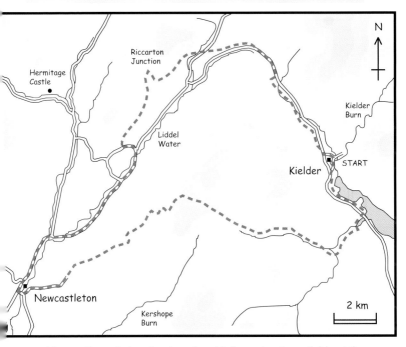

New trails are being developed and information is available at the Visitor Centre and also online. The OS Outdoor Leisure series 1:25000 map for Kielder Water covers not only this area, but also part of the Northumbrian National Park to the east, in great detail – useful for other routes in this guide.

From the castle car park, go downhill and turn left at the bottom to cross the river. This will take you past some houses and then to the right and gently uphill towards the main road. Look out, though, for the Lakeside Way South cycle trail. Follow this for two miles to cross the new footbridge then turn right. This is a well surfaced track which follows the Lewis Burn to The Forks where it swings to the right to follow Akenshaw Burn.

The track rises gently, sometimes through trees, sometimes through clearcut. This is the Bloody Bush Road, built around the 1830s as a route to transport coal from the workings at Lewisburn to the Scottish towns over the border such as Hawick and Jedburgh. It was a toll road, and when you emerge from the trees near the top of Larriston Fells you'll come across the Toll Pillar, which details the charges levied for horses 'leading coals' and other livestock being driven over the route.

The pillar marks the Scottish border. Ahead and to the right is a prominent radio mast. The track has been much improved in recent years and leads fairly easily across the moorland. As you come up to the crest of the fell the views open up to the north and, as they do so, the path joins a forest track. This is the highest point of the route at about 460m.

Follow the track as it heads downhill and round a couple of bends, but look out for a left turn at (545 910) which goes southeast towards Dykecrofts. Join the surfaced road there to roll down into **Newcastleton**. Once a year the town comes alive for the annual Folk Festival in July, but for the rest of the time the impressive main square remains relatively quiet. There are shops and a couple of hotels.

If you're stuck for time, then it's quite possible to simply follow the road back round to Kielder. The route described here, though, attempts to follow the old rail route from Newcastleton to Riccarton Junction – on the way to Hawick – and then from Riccarton Junction along the Border Counties Railway to Kielder. The railway was operational from 1862 but closed in 1956.

While some parts of the old track can be followed almost from the centre of Newcastleton, it comes to a dead-end at the non-existent bridge over Hermitage Water. A more realistic alternative is to take the road out of town for five miles or so to Steeleroad-end. Steele Road was a station, but is now privately owned. You can, however, get access to the old rail route by turning left, back towards Steele Road, and looking out for a track through the trees on the right after a few hundred yards which leads up to the old track.

Contour round Arnton Fell, through trees and cuttings, to emerge into the open and the curiously atmospheric **Riccarton Junction**. It's a strange place, being well away from the nearest road. In the days of rail, it was where the line from Hawick split; one branch going to Newcastleton and the other to Kielder. A group of enthusiasts has spent considerable time and energy restoring some of the old railway buildings here, and they still hope that the Waverley line from Edinburgh to Carlisle may yet be reopened.

Before leaving, take time to go a few yards along the line towards Hawick and, as you come to the trees, you'll notice a small track on the left with a sign for 'Will's Bothy'. Will Ramsbotham was a local climber who was killed in an accident in 1993. The bothy has been renovated and handsomely equipped in his memory, and is open to anyone who wishes to use it. Visitors should, of course, respect the usual 'bothy code' and leave it in at least as good a – if not better – state than they found it.

You're aiming to follow the route to Kielder now, or at least as much of it as you can. It starts off from Riccarton through a cutting and this can get quite wet at times. Stick with it, though, as it emerges on the hillside high above Saughtree giving good views down Liddesdale. The old rail route contours along the side of the hill and eventually, as the road up the valley starts to draw level, you will come across the totally unexpected sight of an old diesel locomotive parked on its very own short section of restored steel rail track. If you were travelling up the road, just a few yards away, you wouldn't even know it was there, as it is completely hidden from view.

The bridge that used to span both the road and the stream is no more, so go down to meet the road. Follow it uphill for a few yards, and there's a grassy track on the right which cuts back up to join the course of the old track through yet another cutting. Again you traverse a hillside, aiming to pass through a forested area for a while to come out on the Kielder road at Myredykes.

It is possible to follow the line of the rail route on the other side of the road now, but this section is fairly overgrown and quite hard work. Instead, it's better to take to the road for a short way until you can join up with the marked cycle route at Deadwater, which brings you back onto the railway to follow it as it leads easily back to **Kielder** village.

32. Langholm

Distance:	27 miles
OS Map:	Landranger 79
Start:	Langholm
Grade:	1
Surface:	road 27 miles

A pleasant route, all on road, exploring part of Eskdale before heading over upland roads to make a circular trail back to the start point. There are no shops on the way, but you can get anything that you need in Langholm and take it with you.

Langholm announces itself as the 'Muckle Toon' – 'muckle' meaning 'big' – and sits at the junction of three rivers, the main one being the Esk. As with many towns in the area, the textile industry has been all but wiped out and the local economy has suffered as a result. Tourism is seen as a way forward, and efforts are being made to develop facilities with this in mind.

At the northern end of the town there's a large car park by the river which provides a convenient starting point. Go towards the town centre and turn right to cross the bridge and head out on the road to Eskdalemuir.

An alternative start can be made if you go to the far end of the car park and cross the stone bridge there signed for the Clan Armstrong centre. Follow the track through the trees and look out for a sign on the left pointing to the Duchess Bridge. The path crosses the bridge over the Esk – an impressive steel structure – then leads to the left to emerge from the trees near a playing field and, from there, along to join the Eskdalemuir road.

Bentpath has an impressive church and, as a diversion, you take the minor road on the other side of the river. Thomas Telford, the famous civil engineer, was born near here in the Meggat Valley. You'll have to re-cross the Esk at the next bridge, as you need to take the road that works its way round to the southwest. There's a bit of a climb coming up shortly, and you should ignore the road on the right for Castle

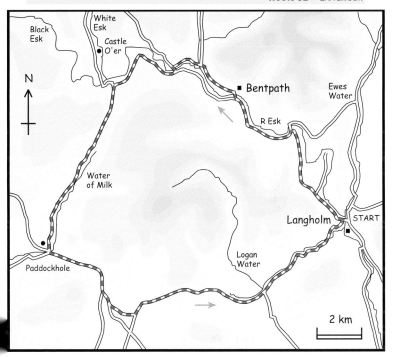

O'er, much as you might prefer the gradient, and press on up the hill. Compensation for your efforts comes in the form of open panoramic views to Chapelcross and the hills of the north Lakes.

Enjoy the roll down to **Paddockhole**, but don't relax too much because there's still some more work to do as you need to cross a watershed at over 220m. It's a fair climb, but from the top you can look forward to a pleasant cruise down the valley as you follow Wauchope Water back to **Langholm**.

33. Scotch Kershope

Distance:	44 miles
OS Maps:	Landranger 79, 80, 86
Start:	Kielder Water
Grade:	5
Surface:	road 15 miles
	track 28 miles
	path 1 mile

One of the bleakest and most remote areas in England lies to the north of Hadrian's Wall, between it and Kielder Water. Vast swathes of moorland and forest with very few roads and minimal habitation characterise the region. This trip follows a section of the Reivers Way C2C route between Kielder and Bewcastle, and then strikes off to take a return leg by way of Paddaburn and northwards over hills and through the heart of the forest.

Navigation is an issue here, particularly on the return leg, and you should aim to be self-sufficient; nor can you yet rely on being able to use a mobile phone in an emergency. The Lime Kiln Inn at Bewcastle does a good bowl of soup, amongst other things, and can be recommended, but there's little else apart from isolated farmhouses. Several fords cross the route and, in particular, the one at Paddaburn leaves you no alternative but to wade the river. In spate this could be problematic; in winter it will certainly be cold.

Has all this managed to put you off yet? Don't let it. It's a tremendous day out, and I have two good reasons to remember doing it for the first time. One, my free-wheel hub suddenly packed up in the middle of the forest – total loss of power; pedal turns but wheel doesn't. Embarrassing? Well just a bit. Some gentle and judicious tapping brought it reluctantly back to life, but would it last the trip? Secondly, I had no idea whether the return leg was going to 'go' or not, so it was a bit of a leap in the dark from that point of view. You don't have the second problem, and I certainly hope you won't have the first…

Dropping towards the Breamish valley, Cheviot Hills (Route 25)

River crossing near Churnsike Lodge, Wark Forest (Routes 33 and 36)

Part of the Open Air Museum at Beamish (Route 39)

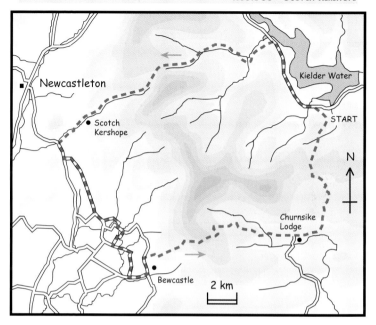

Kielder is an awkward place to get to, particularly from the north. The forest road from near Byrness on the A68 is a possible solution, though there is a nominal fee for using it. I felt that the four miles or so along **Kielder Water** was something I'd rather do at the start of the day than the end. The route comes out onto the lakeside road at (675 868), and if you're travelling by car then you may be able to leave it near here. Alternatively, there is a parking area by the Elf viewpoint at (694 862). Of course, it may suit you to start from Bewcastle instead.

You're aiming for the Lewisburn picnic area and you have the choice of using the road or the purpose-built cycle trail along the southern shore of the lake. There are pros and cons but when you get to Lewisburn, make sure that you don't miss the track leading round to the right as it turns north to follow Akenshaw Burn towards the Bloody Bush road. A mile and a half after crossing the stream, look out for the turn off to the left signed for Kershopefoot.

The route is climbing towards the watershed, but nowhere is it particularly strenuous. Shortly before reaching the highest point of this section — at about 350m – the track ends, and you're now riding on narrow singletrack through the trees. When it swings to the left and heads downhill, look out for a couple of steeper drops which appear quite suddenly if you're travelling at any speed! The wooden bridge over Kershope Burn marks the boundary between Northumberland and Cumbria.

The forest track ambles gently downhill beside the Kershope Burn, and as the valley opens out a little you might be lucky enough to see some of the many deer that live in the area. **Scotch Kershope** is on the left and used to be an LEA outdoor centre. People I know who have stayed there speak fondly of the midges, and it's easy to see why…

Eventually this leisurely jaunt meets a road at Kershope Bridge, and a rude awakening waits as you turn left to pull up a steep and tortuous hill. The gradient eases, but there's still work to do as each downhill is accompanied by a corresponding uphill stretch. At the bottom of a long descent, turn left for Woodside and notice that you're still following the Reivers Way route number '10' signs – for the moment, anyway. This is much more rural in character, the lanes here are very narrow and you'll pass through a number of gates.

Shortly after passing Croft, cross a stream and turn right; this is a departure from the normal C2C route. Follow the lanes round past Crook, through a couple of fords and eventually reaching **Bewcastle**. The castle is partly hidden behind some trees and there's a church to the right. The churchyard itself is home to the famous Bewcastle Cross, mentioned in the Spadeadam route description and which is well worth a few minutes of your time.

Take the road heading up the hill alongside a line of windswept hawthorn trees. Eventually the gradient eases, and you can continue more easily to Crossgreens. Turn right here on a track leading steadily upwards and over open moorland. As you gain height the views in all directions are quite stunning, and there's a real feeling that you're heading into remote country. And, of course, you are.

On the skyline ahead is the edge of the forest. When you reach it, go through the gate and turn left – the route to the south leads into a restricted MOD area, so there's no access in that direction. The track has a good surface here and, while there's still a little more work to do, you'll soon come across some tremendous downhill sections. The route

St Cuthbert's church at Bewcastle

heads generally west, and there are no real problems navigating along this section.

Emerging into more open country, you'll find yourself having to deal with the ford at Paddaburn. There's no way round it and, likely as not, the simplest way is to take your shoes off and just paddle through it.

Continue easily now to **Churnsike Lodge**; ignore a turning to the left after half a mile – this leads to Padda Crag. When you reach the lodge turn left to pass to the north of it. At Whitehill the track turns to the north and soon passes the prominent Muckle Samuel's Crags – there must surely be a story here – on the left. Pass a track to the left shortly and continue to ride north.

The trail swings to the left and slightly downhill towards a junction at (683 803). Turn right and go a little way uphill to a T-junction at (685 806). Be sure to turn left here; if you don't, you'll pass the entrance to a quarry and this means you've gone wrong. The trail turns to the north and climbs for a while before turning left to drop down to a junction at (674 812). If you've got this far then you can relax because all the hard work is done. You should be getting glimpses of Kielder Water in the distance.

Head north just a few yards, and you'll find a small sign indicating a memorial cairn to one 'Lord Robinson, Baron of Kielder Forest and Adelaide'. In fact, Roy Robinson – later to be knighted – was closely involved in the inception of the Forestry Commission just after the First World War and in its further development for over thirty years after that, in one capacity or another, before his sudden death. His memorial cairn is up on the hill to the right.

Some pleasant cruising now and, although there are trails leading off to the right and left, the main route should be pretty obvious. There's a junction at (686 848). Take the track leading northwest, and this aims directly down to meet the road, about half a mile to the east of the Calvert Trust Centre. If you're feeling in need of refreshment – and you've surely earned it – then the nearest pub is in Falstone village, just a little way past the dam.

34. Lower Redesdale

Distance:	**24 miles**
OS Maps:	**Landranger 80, 81**
Start:	**Bellingham**
Grade:	**3**
Surface:	**road 17.5 miles**
	track 5.5 miles
	path 1 mile

This follows Lower Redesdale for a while before climbing to about 300m on forest tracks. You then take some upland roads and circle round for a fine run down to Redesmouth and back to the start in Bellingham. In places you follow the Reivers Way cycle route, and in others the Border County Ride.

Bellingham is a pleasant town with a number of pubs and shops, and it is the focus for a number of long-distance trails. The Pennine Way, the Reivers Way and the Border County Ride all pass through. The first

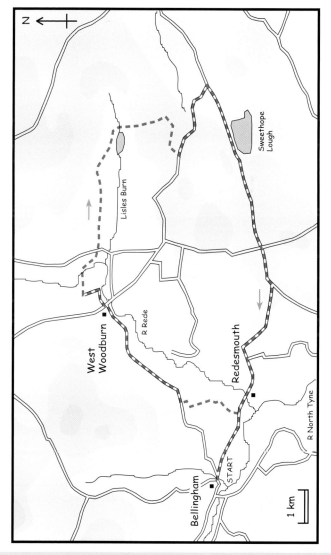

of these is a walkers' route and the latter for horse riders. All of them, however, can be used by cyclists at some point or other. There is a campsite half a mile or so out of the town, and there's plenty of scope for exploration in the area.

Take the road out of **Bellingham** towards Redesdale. After about a mile or so it passes under an old rail bridge, and just a few yards further on there's track off to the left signed for both the Border County Ride and also the C2C Reivers Way. The track heads uphill, and as the gradient levels out you need to look out for a gate at (864 833) signed, but not obviously so, for the Ride. If you miss the gate, you'll end up at the old Rede Bridge and will need to retrace your steps.

Go through the gate to follow a vague track over the grassy hillside heading northeast. After just a few yards, though, and as the horse riders' route continues in that direction, you need to strike off northwest towards Rawfoot, which will soon come into view. This is a bridleway, though by no means an obvious one, and you have every right to use it. Aim to the left of the farm buildings, kink right to pass between them, then take the farm track which goes up to meet the road.

Of course, you could simply have taken the other road out of Bellingham to get here, but then you'd have missed all the fun…

The road to **West Woodburn** is on an easy gradient, and there's a pub that does bar meals and snacks if, that is, your conscience will allow it at such an early stage of the trip. In any event turn left along the main road, but almost immediately take a right turn down a narrow lane through the village.

Decision time now. The road leads east to Townhead and some stepping stones across the river. If you're feeling adventurous you might want to take a look, but my feeling is that in anything but the driest season it could be a bit problematic. Instead, I took a left turn at Yellow House farm and went along the lane to join a track leading to the rather elegant East Woodburn Bridge.

You're back on the Border County Ride route as it follows the river before heading up to a crossroads. Go straight across, climbing gently as the views unfold. The track turns left and aims for a gap in the skyline. In fact, you're following a bridleway now, and it turns right at (930 872) to run alongside a stone wall. This is quite rough to start with, but soon turns into a grassy path – at least the gradient is on your side.

You reach the junction of two stone walls at (935 868). Some older maps show this as the corner of a wood, but it has since been clearcut.

Signs for the bridleway take you through a gate with a stone dyke to your right. Don't follow that, but look instead for a gap in the wall where a good track follows along the other side of it.

Very shortly you'll reach a red dirt track. Turn right down the track, but only for a few yards, then go left heading generally eastwards. Maps show that the bridleway crosses and re-crosses the forest track, but this is a bit of a clearcut wilderness and there is little choice but to stick with the track as it passes to the left of a conspicuous lake. This is no bad thing, though, as it's an easy gradient right up to the high point of 292m by a small quarry.

Heading downhill, follow round to the right, and the trail should bring you out at Summit Cottages, which are situated on the course of an old rail line. Take the track up to join the road and cruise along the road and round towards **Sweethope Lough**. As you approach the lough, you can pick out the top of Great Whanney Crag over to the right. One of the approaches to the crag runs along the edge of the forest up ahead.

The road trends gently upwards as it moves into open country and along towards the main A68. At this point the main road is following the course of the old Roman Dere Street as it forced a route north in no uncertain manner. Cross straight over, though, and enjoy the views as you look forward to a long and effortless roll down to **Redesmouth** and back to **Bellingham**.

35. Stamfordham

Distance:	**36 miles/37 miles**
OS Maps:	**Landranger 81, 87, 88**
Start:	**Kirkwhelpington**
Grade:	**2**
Surface:	**road 33.5 miles/37 miles**
	track 2.5 miles

A pleasant ramble through varied Northumbrian countryside and passing through quiet villages, this route is for the most part on easy gradients. There is an off-road section, but this can be avoided if you prefer.

Start in the village of **Kirkwhelpington** and head downhill to follow alongside the River Wansbeck for a while as it meanders through pastures. The road veers away from the river and, after a mile or so, meets the B6342 just to the north of **Wallington Hall**, built in 1688 and said to be one of Northumberland's finest stately homes.

The Wallington estate spreads on both sides of the road, and the house and grounds are now owned by the National Trust. There's an information kiosk in the car park on the right, and you may want to spend a little time looking around. The elegant clock tower is quite unusual. To the left of the road, and just past the car park, a woodland walk leads to an ornamental walled garden and conservatory. As an aside, note that 'Capability' Brown, who designed gardens at Blenheim Palace and Kew – amongst others, was born a couple of miles away at Kirkharle.

Moving on, the road heads downhill towards Paine's Bridge, which crosses the Wansbeck. Turn left just before the bridge and then right after a mile to cross the river further downstream and climb towards **Bolam Country Park** – you'll pass Bolam Lake on your left. A quarter of a mile or so before reaching the main A696 Newcastle road, look out for a right turn signposted for Stamfordham. This road heads westwards and crosses the main road just to the north of **Belsay Castle**, which can be seen over to the left.

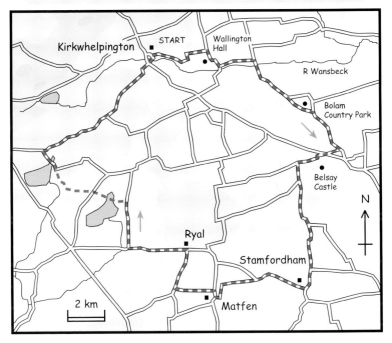

The route turns south and takes a gently undulating line all the way to Stamfordham, a picturesque village with a spacious green and a couple of pubs. Quiet roads lead easily past Fenwick and along to the almost unnaturally tidy village of **Matfen**. You're actually following the Reivers Cycle Route for a few miles as it weaves a course from Tynemouth on the east coast to Whitehaven on the west coast.

There's a bit of a climb now as you head towards Ryal, a small settlement situated on a bleak and windswept hilltop. The Reivers route takes an off-road section through West Side farm and down a grassy track to rejoin the road at Hallington. The track, however, can get a tad boggy if there has been recent rain, so can only really be recommended in dry weather. If you choose to go that way, then look out for a gate on the right as you go west from the crossroads at **Ryal**.

Staying with the road means that you get a fine run downhill for

Off-road section of the route, near Little Swinburn farm

about a mile and a half. The downside is that there's a bit of a climb now up to Hallington. After half a mile or so look out for a track on the left which leads over towards Hallington Reservoir. Follow it to cross the reservoir by a causeway and go on to meet the B6342. Another track continues straight ahead towards Little Swinburn, where you rejoin a surfaced road leading easily to Colt Crag Reservoir.

This section on tracks can be avoided by staying on the road to Little Bavington and then taking the minor road through Throckrington to rejoin the route near the reservoir, adding an extra mile onto the total.

Soon after the reservoir, take the right turn signposted for **Kirkwhelpington**. This is superb open upland scenery with good views to the north as the road takes an easy line across country before dropping down to the village and back to your start point.

36. Spadeadam

Distance:	29 miles
OS Map:	**Landranger 86**
Start:	**Gilsland**
Grade:	3
Surface:	road 21 miles
	track 8 miles

This route wends a path through part of Hadrian's Wall country and also runs through part of the remote Spadeadam Forest. The forest track can't be avoided, but it is on a good surface. There is also a river crossing, and there's really no option here other than to get wet feet.

The village of Gilsland is on the course of the Roman wall, and in former years was popular as a spa resort. The novelist Sir Walter Scott proposed to his future wife at the 'Popping Stone', which can still be seen in the grounds of the Spa Hotel. To the north of Gilsland is a Ministry of Defence restricted area which covers much of Spadeadam Forest. The route circumnavigates this area, so don't be surprised to see or hear the occasional movements of military helicopters.

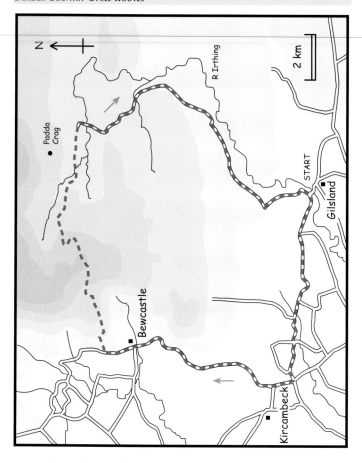

Head west from **Gilsland** for about five miles to a crossroads where you can turn right for Bewcastle. In fact, this section of the route is following part of the 'Reivers Way', a coast to coast cycle route running between Tynemouth on the east coast and Maryport on the west.

Bewcastle is north of the Roman Wall, so it's a bit of a mystery why a fort was built here, especially when it doesn't appear to occupy a particularly strategic position, being situated, as it is, in a valley. Nowadays the area is isolated and remote, but at one time there were several routes crossing the border hereabouts, and Bewcastle was a hub of reiving activity in those turbulent and lawless years.

Next to the fort is St Cuthbert's church and its famous Bewcastle Cross dating from the 7th or 8th century. The cross is missing its top section, but is inscribed with carvings and runes and is said to mark the burial place of the Anglo Saxon King Alcfrith. A small stone building in the grounds of the church is home to an exhibition of local history and folklore.

Climb from **Bewcastle** in a fairly unremitting manner to reach Crossgreens, where a track off to the right leads towards the forest. The gradient is easier, and you pass through one or two gates, advancing further into this isolated area. Look back to catch views of the Lake District.

As the track approaches the forested area it swings round to the right to reach a gate. Go through it and take the track to the left, heading east. It undulates a little, but now trends generally downhill and at times through open areas. You are aiming to cross Tarn Beck by a ford at (645 773), and, unless you are really lucky, the easiest way is to walk through it in bare feet.

Half a mile further on is a junction, and a mile to the north of this is **Padda Crag**. If you want to detour and have a look at it, then the last quarter mile has access by foot – follow a small stream that heads directly north towards the crag. It's a pleasant spot and a sun-trap on a hot day.

Your route carries on past the junction to reach Churnside Lodge and rejoin a tarred road. There's a little bit more work to do as the road loosely follows the course of the River Irthing as it works its way towards **Gilsland**, passing the main entrance to the MOD base a mile or two before the village.

37. Vindolanda

Distance:	32 miles
OS Map:	Landranger 87
Start:	Fourstones
Grade:	3
Surface:	road 27 miles
	track 5 miles

A tour through some classic Hadrian's Wall country – what was once the edge of the Roman Empire – and an excursion through remote Wark Forest make this a fine trip. The off-road section can't realistically be avoided, although the surface for the most part is good.

The village of **Fourstones** lies on the course of the Stanegate Roman road which connected the line of forts situated along it, the most notable of these being Vindolanda. You can't fail to notice the wooden church, built by an enthusiastic minister at his own expense and still referred to locally as 'The Mission'.

Cycle west from the village to pass through Newbrough, and it's here that the long and fairly relentless climb begins; it isn't particularly steep, but the novelty soon wears off. Eventually the gradient eases and the prominent remains of the Roman fort at Housesteads can be seen over to the right.

Grindon Lough, which curiously doesn't appear to have any obvious outlet, is a wildlife sanctuary. About a mile and a half past the lough the road kinks left downhill quite steeply. You can see Vindolanda straight ahead. Don't pick up speed here because you need to turn off to the right and go even more steeply down to a small parking area. This is the east entrance to the site, but there's another one further on. Take the track to the right of some farm buildings up another steep, but short, hill. The surface soon improves, and you'll find the west entrance to **Vindolanda** on your left.

The site, of course, has a rich history, and if you have time then it's well worth looking around and visiting the museum.

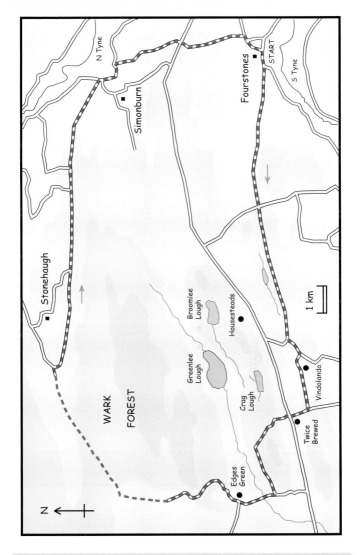

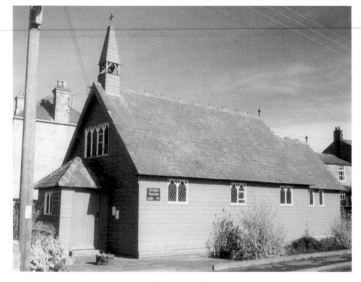

St Aidan's church, Fourstones

Reach a T-junction after a mile and turn right. You are now entering the national park, and there's a visitor centre just as you meet the main road at the oddly named **Twice Brewed**. Along the main road is the Twice Brewed Inn. It seems, or so the story goes, that General Wade passed this way in 1745 with his army. They were trying to cut off Bonnie Prince Charlie who was advancing on Carlisle as part of the uprising. Wade stopped at the inn but found the beer too weak and told the publican to take it away and brew again. Hence the name 'Twice Brewed Inn'...

Go straight across the main road, climbing up to cross Hadrian's Wall itself. There are fine views of Peel Crag and Crag Lough over to the right. The wall stretches into the distance to the west and also to the east, running along the tops of the crags. In all it traverses the country for over 70 miles from the Solway Firth to Wallsend on the Tyne and was a considerable feat of engineering. The sections here are particularly well preserved and give a good indication of what was involved.

Pass the parking area then follow the road round to a T-junction to turn right for **Edges Green** and on towards Wark Forest. This is hilly country, and there's a lot of up and down as you weave your way up, over and around them. The character of the area also changes, and the landscape takes on a more remote feel to it, as indeed it is – there's virtually no habitation for many miles to the north.

The tarred road stops at the edge of the forest and you're on a track now. I've been here in winter when the ruts were just at that annoying depth that catches your pedals, and the wheels were also breaking through ice in the puddles that form in them. At the same time the track between the ruts was just too soft to give a decent surface. Hard work, but in drier weather it's OK, and in any event the surface improves after a mile and a half at Grindon Green.

There is some more gentle uphill before heading down to Whygate, where you rejoin the road and a tarred surface. Take the road up through trees, which brings you out on Broadpool Common with good views to the north. This is fairly easy going, and you'll pass Ravensheugh Crags and then have a long roll down to meet the B6320. The remains of St Mungo's 13th-century church are nearby towards **Simonburn**.

Stay on the main road for half a mile, then turn right and uphill – it's the last one – for a mile or so to the B6318. This is on the course of Hadrian's Wall, again near the site of Milecastle 29. From here it's downhill virtually all the way back to **Fourstones**.

38. Tyne Valley

Distance:	31 miles
OS Maps:	Landranger 87, 88
Start:	Rowlands Gill
Grade:	2
Surface:	road 15 miles
	track 16 miles

Two main features of this route are the River Tyne, or at least the part of it that you cycle along, and the Derwent Walk, which, despite its name, is also a cycling route. The link between them crosses hills from the Tyne to the Derwent Valley and, all in all, the route works well and has a lot to offer. It's easily accessible from Newcastle city centre by following the Keelman's Way cycle route along the south bank of the Tyne. The Swalwell Visitor Centre at Blaydon is also a good place to start – see the Beamish route for details of its location. Just to be different, though, it is described here from Rowlands Gill.

There is a campsite in **Rowlands Gill**, and following signs to it will bring you to a large car park at (168 585), just by the entrance to the campsite. The Derwent Walk cycle route – which, incidentally, forms part of the Sustrans Coast to Coast route – runs through the town. To find it, go up the hill from the car park and you'll see that the cycle route goes along the pavement here towards a petrol station. Just past the petrol station the route veers off to the right onto the old rail line.

From Rowlands Gill to **Blaydon** on the rail route is a real breeze, passing through woodland and over Nine Arches Viaduct to leave the River Derwent down to your left. At the end of the rail line you'll emerge onto a fairly busy road just by an access lane to Blaydon Rugby Club. Diagonally over the main road, and to your left, is a minor road, and if you look carefully you should see a blue and white 'C2C' sign as you're still following the Coast to Coast route at this point.

Take the minor road, and the signs will point you onto a path round to the right. Cross the River Derwent by a pedestrian suspension bridge and follow the track passing under the main A1 road. Stay with the left bank of the Derwent as the path goes under another road and then under a rail bridge to reach the mighty River Tyne just where the Derwent empties its own contribution into it.

The main road and rail bridges into Newcastle city centre are some miles downstream but you can see three bridges upstream. The one furthest away carries the A1. The nearest one is the Scotswood steel suspension bridge and the one that we're going to use. In between these two is an abandoned rail bridge. There's a cycle route going over the Scotswood bridge which links NCR14 on the south bank and NCR72 on the north.

Pick up NCR72 over the river as it heads west parallel to the main road, and then underneath the A1. The Tyne is over to your left and you should follow the cycle route over the new bridge into the recently developed waterfront area alongside the river.

A little further on, just by Newburn Bridge, is the Boathouse Inn with marks on the building to show the levels of some of the great Tyne

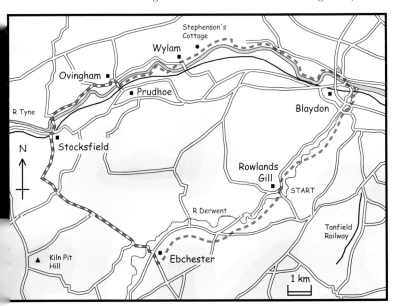

floods. We're entering the Tyne Riverside Country Park and there's a visitor centre just up ahead.

A cycle path follows the riverbank for half a mile before turning away from the river to pass some cottages. Turn left to join the route of the Wylam Waggonway, one of the oldest railways in the country, which used to carry coal from local mines. George Stephenson was one of the early pioneers of steam locomotives, and the cottage where he was born in 1781 is on the right, just after the golf course. It's just under a mile to the picturesque village of **Wylam**, and you might want to spend a little time looking around.

Stay with the rail route as it passes under a road and then over the Tyne on an old steel bridge. The track used to join the main rail line here. Turn right by some redbrick houses and head off down a tarred track, signed as a cycle route for Prudhoe, which follows the riverbank. Cycling through the trees here, there's the distinctive scent of the wild garlic that carpets the area. The track ends in a car park by a curious pair of bridges; there is a single-lane road for traffic and a separate bridge for pedestrians. Choose one of them and cross it to reach **Ovingham**, then take a left turn to follow the north bank of the river. Gazing over the river to the south will give you an idea of the hills that you're going to have to tackle sooner or later.

Cross the Tyne at the next bridge and cycle up to meet the main road through **Stocksfield**. Turn right then almost immediately left to head steeply uphill. The gradient eases after a while, the road takes a sharp left turn and then climbs steeply again to reach a pub on the top of the hill. Enjoy the views back into the Tyne Valley as you catch your breath. This is part of the old Roman Dere Street, which took an uncompromising line from York to the Firth of Forth, crossing the Tyne at nearby Corbridge. Relax on the long downhill towards **Ebchester**; but not for too long, because there's a short, but quite brutal, haul up to the main road there.

Once again, turn right and almost immediately left to climb out of the town. It isn't as bad as it looks, though, because you're only going as far as where the old rail line – now the Derwent Walk – crosses the road as it contours the hillside. In fact, this was Ebchester Station, and its situation offers fine views over the valley. There's a small picnic area and an interpretive plaque outlining the history of the town from Roman times.

So all the hard work's done, and you can savour the five miles rolling gently downhill to Rowlands Gill as the route passes through

Old rail bridge over the Tyne near Wylam

both woodland and open country and also over three viaducts in the process. Approaching **Rowlands Gill**, the Gibside Estate, once owned by George Bowes who made his fortune from coal in the 18th century, is over to the right. The prominent monument that you can see rising above the trees was given the unassuming title of the Column of British Liberty. Gibside Hall and other buildings in the landscaped estate are now in the care of the National Trust, and give a particular perspective on the Industrial Revolution if you have the time to visit.

39. Beamish

Distance:	31 miles
OS Map:	Landranger 88
Start:	Blaydon
Grade:	2
Surface:	road 2 miles
	track 28.5 miles
	path 0.5 mile

This is a tremendous route and full of interest as it weaves a curious line through parts of the industrial northeast. It scarcely touches roads, but instead makes use of old rail routes that are now cycleways, all of which have good surfaces and easy gradients. There is one very short section early on in the trip where you'll need to push, but, other than that, the going is surprisingly easy. The route passes by Beamish Open Air Museum and also the Tanfield Railway, which claims to be the oldest in the world.

Swalwell Visitor Centre has leaflets on local points of interest, including the Derwent Valley Walk, which forms part of this route. The visitor centre is just by the side of **Blaydon** Rugby Club and is located at (199 619). There is a parking area here. The route is also accessible from Newcastle city centre by following the Keelman's Way and/or the C2C route along the Tyne. The Metro Centre rail link is just a short distance away.

Access to the Derwent Valley Walk is just behind the visitor centre. It's an old rail route, and the line heads along the side of a hill through trees with the river down to your right. Even travelling only a few yards, it seems as though you're a world away from the urban sprawl that you've just left.

After just over a mile you're looking for a track off to the left through the woods. It's signed for 'Clockburn Lonnen' and heads upwards, steeply at first, but the gradient soon eases. Turn left onto an unsurfaced road which takes you up to a T-junction.

Turn right and go up the hill for about half a mile. Just as you reach a pub on the left there's a bridleway signed for Sunniside. It goes across open country then winds round the backs of some houses to meet a road. Go straight across on a path signed for **Tanfield Railway**. The railway, used originally to bring minerals down to the Tyne, has been restored, and steam trains run a regular service – a popular feature of the railway is Causey Arch, a bridge constructed over a gorge in spectacular surroundings.

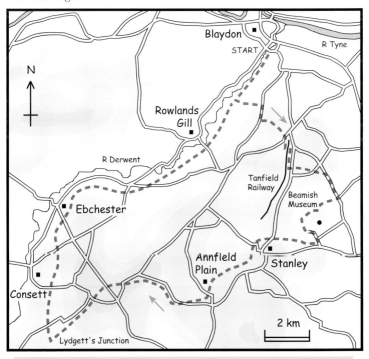

The smelter wagon at Lydgett's Junction near Consett

When you reach the railway turn right to follow it. After a short distance, cross the line via a gate and follow the path on the east side to Tanfield Station. Cross the main road and head off down a track signed for 'Birkheads Lane'; this soon turns into singletrack and is, in fact, the course of yet another railway. When you reach a road go straight across. At the next road turn right and go downhill for a while until you come to a left turn for Kibblesworth. Don't take it, but instead turn right here on a track which goes down through some woods round the back of **Beamish Museum**, glimpses of which you can see through the trees, then down to meet a road at Beamish Hall. Turn left, go up the hill and you're now at the entrance to the museum.

To do Beamish justice you really need to spend some time there. The entrance fee entitles you to use the trams to get from one part of the museum to the next. There's a lot to see so allow plenty of time if you're going in.

Head towards the main road, passing a pub over on your left. You're looking for a path on the left down to the Consett and Sunderland Cycle Route, again an old rail track. Turn right to pass under the bridge, and you'll not fail to miss the sculptures of browsing cattle made out of old mechanical parts. You'll come across more sculptures along the route, but better to discover them for yourself.

At **Annfield Plain** cross the road by the supermarket, but after a few yards the route leaves the rail track through a gap in the stone wall. Follow along the road, and you'll come across a newly built bridge over a main road. Shortly you'll reach an ornamental pond with some industrial units over to the right. Turn right on the road, then almost immediately left on another path through some shrubbery. The track parallels a main road for a while before going through some 'S' bends to emerge at a roundabout. Aim for the car park of the Jolly Drovers pub to pick up the route again to Leadgate.

Follow the track alongside some playing fields; you're fairly high up now, and there are extensive views to the south and to the Pennines. Cross some waste ground and a road to head for a roundabout and yet more sculptures. Pass these and go along to **Lydgett's Junction** – the smelter wagon – where the Waskerley Way, the Derwent Walk and the Lanchester Valley Walk all meet.

Turn right onto the Derwent Walk, heading for Consett. Cross a main road, then you're up on an open grassy crest which leads along through the edge of **Consett**, past a cemetery and onto the old rail track. From here it's an absolute breeze for 10 miles back to Swalwell, gently downhill all the way and crossing several viaducts. There's a slight deviation when you get to **Rowlands Gill**. Take the footpath on the right side of the road – it's well signed – then rejoin the rail track just past a petrol station.

All credit should go to those councils, other organisations and individuals who had the foresight to appreciate that these rail tracks – even when closure is forced upon them – are indeed an asset to be cherished, and not a commodity to be sold off for short-term gain.

40. Deerness Valley

Distance:	**35 miles**
OS Maps:	**Landranger 87(only briefly), 88, 92**
Start:	**Lanchester**
Grade:	**3**
Surface:	**road 9 miles**
	track 26 miles

A superb route that, for the most part, uses old rail tracks that have been converted and made accessible to cyclists and walkers. The area's industrial past included supplying iron ore and coal from local pits, and the railways were used to transport it. Nowadays, of course, the pits have closed and the railways have gone. Fortunately part of that legacy has been preserved, and we can at least use what remains for recreational purposes. Our route uses the Lanchester Valley Walk, the Deerness Valley Walk and just a short section on the Waskerley Way.

Lanchester's history goes back to Roman times. It was on the route of Dere Street, and the remains of the fort that was built here can still be seen just a little way to the southwest of the town. It stands on private land, but can be viewed from the road where there is an interpretive board. The railway through the town used to run between Consett and Durham, and the old station is still standing. Access to the track is staightforward.

Take the trail out of **Lanchester** heading southeast down the valley. After a mile or so it crosses the River Browney and, like the river, ambles in a quiet and leisurely way through farms and fields. A couple of miles after passing through **Langley Park** you'll see some ruins over to the left, and these are marked on the map and named **Bear Park**. In fact this has nothing to do with bears, but is a corruption of the old French 'beau repaire', meaning beautiful retreat. It was the country seat of the monks of Durham founded in the 13th century by Prior Bertram. It seems, however, that the prior's manor was destroyed by invading Scots around 1640. The nearby former pit village of Bearpark takes the same name.

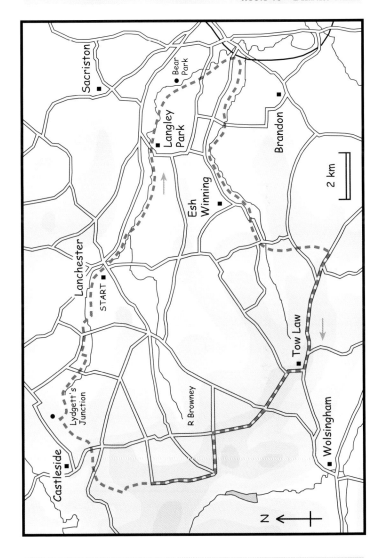

The route passes under an old stone bridge, and this is the junction where the line used to join the main rail line, which still runs north through Durham and up the east coast. The Lanchester Valley Walk stops here, but you're now at a junction where it meets the Deerness Valley Walk and also the Brandon/Bishop Auckland Walk.

Turn west into the Deerness Valley, as the old line goes through cuttings and along the hillside. Brandon is over to the left, and already this valley has taken on completely different characteristics to the Lanchester Valley. The sides of the valley are steeper, there are more trees and it's a little more intimate, a little more enclosed. It isn't a dead-end, and there is a road along it, but it just seems more tranquil somehow.

Rather like following a canal towpath, cycling a rail route gives a quite distinct perspective to towns and villages in comparison to making the same journey through them by road. Maybe it's because you see the backs of houses rather than the fronts; peering almost voyeuristically into people's private back gardens rather than their more public facades?

Approaching **Esh Winning**, you pass through woodland, alongside a stream and through meadows to edge round the south of the village. Again, the place is associated with its colliery, which was opened in 1859. It was described as a 'model colliery village', and in 1894 it was written that 'The houses, built on the south side of the road are really all that could be desired. A large garden is attached to each house, to be cultivated as the pleasure of the occupants dictates' (F. Whelan, *History, Topography and Directory of Durham*).

The route moves further up the valley and crosses a couple of minor roads. The second of these is by a phone box and children's play area. After this, the trail starts to climb and, as railways go, this is surprisingly steep; so much so, that you wonder how trains got up it at all. Cyclists are made of sterner stuff, though, and quickly warm to the challenge.

Turn right when you reach the road and enjoy the views across Weardale as you head along to join the B6299 towards Tow Law. There's a church at the junction, and I had to look twice at some curiously shaped, and what appear to be ceramic, 'headstones' in the churchyard. Is this a peculiarly local fashion? Well perhaps, because there are more of them when you pass through **Tow Law**, a little further on. I've never seen any like them before or since.

Join the main road, then, as it leads through Tow Law and on towards Consett. This is open moorland, and you need to stay with the main road as far as Drover House, where there's a left turn for Salters Gate. A mile or so along here and the road swings to the north. Again, there are extensive views across the heather-covered upland. Oxen Law is an abandoned farmhouse at a crossroads. A track heads north from here and soon turns into a grassy path. It goes through a gate and can get a little boggy in wet weather. It leads fairly quickly, though, round to the left and down to join the Waskerley Way, a well-surfaced cycle track and part of the Coast to Coast route.

This is a fairly remote spot, but despite that, when we arrived there were signs advertising some tearooms nearby where you are assured of a 'friendly welcome from Margaret'. Whether you choose to embrace her welcome or not, the track here is quite superb as it you speed along the hillside crossing a couple of roads, pass Rowley Station and cross a breathtaking viaduct to arrive at the smelter wagon at **Lydgett's Junction**. The junction is where the Waskerley Way links with the Lanchester Valley Walk, the Consett to Sunderland cycle route and the Derwent Valley cycle route. The smelter wagon is a symbolic reminder of the former steel works at Consett.

Take the route as it leads easily into the Lanchester Valley. There is a minor detour around a section of farmland at one point, but then the route rejoins the railway just after Harbuck Cottages. It crosses the river by a fine bridge, and a little further along the hillside you pass under Accommodation Bridge – rather unusual and originally purpose-built to allow livestock to cross the line. It's a short ride from here back into **Lanchester**.

LISTING OF CICERONE GUIDES

For full and up-to-date information
on our ever expanding list of guides,
please visit our website:
www.cicerone.co.uk.

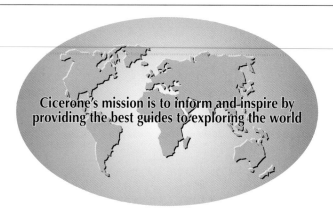

Cicerone's mission is to inform and inspire by providing the best guides to exploring the world

Since its foundation 40 years ago, Cicerone has specialised in publishing guidebooks and has built a reputation for quality and reliability. It now publishes nearly 300 guides to the major destinations for outdoor enthusiasts, including Europe, UK and the rest of the world.

Written by leading and committed specialists, Cicerone guides are recognised as the most authoritative. They are full of information, maps and illustrations so that the user can plan and complete a successful and safe trip or expedition – be it a long face climb, a walk over Lakeland fells, an alpine cycling tour, a Himalayan trek or a ramble in the countryside.

With a thorough introduction to assist planning, clear diagrams, maps and colour photographs to illustrate the terrain and route, and accurate and detailed text, Cicerone guides are designed for ease of use and access to the information.

If the facts on the ground change, or there is any aspect of a guide that you think we can improve, we are always delighted to hear from you.

Cicerone Press
2 Police Square Milnthorpe Cumbria LA7 7PY
Tel: 015395 62069 Fax: 015395 63417
info@cicerone.co.uk www.cicerone.co.uk

CICERONE